THE ROLE OF AN INTERCESSOR

VOL II

THE STRATEGIST

PRESENTED BY
DR. LOVELLA MOGERE AND COLLABORATIVE

THE ROLE OF AN INTERCESSOR

The Strategist

Vol II

Presented By

Dr Lovella Mogere & Collaborative

Nous Mass Media products are available at special quantity discounts for bulk purchase for sales promotions, premiums, fund-raising, and educational needs. For details, email Nous Mass Media at nousmassmedia@gmail.com or call 832-598-8608.

The Role of An Intercessor Vol II - The Strategist by Lovella Mogere, Jamisha Alford, Quentina Attipoe, Alana Bell, Jessie Burts, Kellie Hennings, Julie Hitchens, Trave' Hunter, Shanaire Hunter, Wanda Gentry, Yeleina Morgan, Zandra Osborne, Sheneki White and Veranda Williams by Nous Mass Media.

Table of Contents

Introduction **7**

Chapter 1 **11**
The Grand Strategy 11

Chapter 2 **19**
A Rewarding Journey 19

Chapter 3 **28**
After The Armor 28

Chapter 4 **39**
The Effective Strategy of the Kingdom Tactician 39

Chapter 5 **51**
Arise To Battle 51

Chapter 6 **63**
The Heart Of An Intercessor 63

Chapter 7 **78**
Preventing A Breach 78

Chapter 8 **89**
Engage In Spiritual Warfare 90

Chapter 9 **99**
The Rules of Engagement 99

Chapter 10 **113**
It's About to Go Down!!! 113

Chapter 11 **125**
Warrior's Arsenal 126

Chapter 12 **146**
Attack By Stratagem 146

Chapter 13 **158**
The Strategies Of A Militant Warrior 159

Chapter 14 **167**
The Strategy of the Beloved 167

Introduction

Tacticians, your prayers establish ruling against the opposing forces of darkness that conspire to overtake you in your time of weakness. It is your decrees and declarations that depose your enemies without relent. Arise! Mobilize! It's time to dethrone what comes as an authority to dominate your soul.

You tactician, are a strategist, skilled in the art of war. God armed you with the sword, the Word of God, to stand against the enemy's tactics. He equipped you with strength, wisdom, and discernment through His own Spirit to stay strong in the spiritual battle. God invites you to spend time in His Presence, through prayer and worship, pressing in to know Him more. It's in your prayers that you learn God's concepts - *His mind*, God's theory - *His word*, God's plans - *His design*, God's action - *His movement*, and God's policy - *His system*.

Though the warfare may be physically and psychologically oriented, principles of strategy still apply. *"The weapons we fight with are not the weapons of the world. On the contrary, they have divine power to demolish strongholds".* 2 Corinthians 10:4 However, you are able to formulate strategies. How? Through prayers, worship and your Intercession. The strategies are given to process to take advantage of God's wisdom to overcome the enemy.

The answer to your prayers lies within the confluence between you and God, your capabilities resolve and strategize the outcome of your spiritual warfare. *"Behold, I have given you authority to tread on serpents and scorpions, and over all the power of the enemy and nothing shall hurt you."* Luke 10:19. God has given you power!

Detail Assessment and Planning

Explores the fundamental factors (the way, seasons, terrain, leadership, and management) and seven elements that determine the outcomes of military engagements. By thinking, assessing, and comparing these points, a commander can calculate his chances of victory

DR. LOVELLA MOGERE

Chapter 1

The Grand Strategy

To those alert and awakened, though you have eyes to see, and know the sequential time of the Creator, you are needed like never before. For the art and language of the ancient war needs to be thought to the minds of war. For the emerging are discovering the warrior within, yet question themselves and realize that they have lived in the shadows of the tacticians that went before them. Their faith has been tested, by illusions and deceptive mental onslaughts. Though the tactician, in search of the sound that echoes of the generals of our past that pierce through our future, you, emerging, are the voice of our present that penetrates to tomorrow.

The Creator is raising up warriors, who are a strategist, skilled in the art of war. A warrior specialized in combat, especially in intercession but hidden within the context of the economic, trade, finance, trade, military, or academic culture society that recognizes a separate warrior class or caste.

The Warrior Culture

Every warrior lives in a warrior culture, which focuses on the practice and refinement of martial methods to achieve some end for that society.

The Role of the Warrior

The warrior sacrifices himself for the good of others. His task is to take care of the elderly, the defenseless, those who cannot provide for themselves, and above all, the children - the future of humanity.

The Warrior's Mindset

The warriors' thoughts are more than aggressive and

determined. It is about overcoming challenges and adversities. It's about mental possessing, understanding, and being able to utilize a set of psychological and physical skills that allow someone to be effective, adaptive, and persistent.

Warriors have built on the past efforts of strategies, led by voices that guide to advance the kingdom of God's policy/**pol'-i-si** (*strategema, strategeo*). There's a new generation of warriors, thinkers, strategists, economics, academics, and policymakers that are not constrained by spiritual war concepts, but rather provide fresh insight into strategic, and alternative, ways to promote the Kingdom's agenda. In doing so, cultural norms are broken, the invisible gateways and portals are now visible, the squatter unseen, that has set up traps and snares to confront and contend against you in the trenches are now visible.

The episodes of war and human conflicts are persistent when it comes to the rich tapestry of the art of war. And in such a vast ambit of wanton destruction there have been a few civilizations, tribes and factions that had accepted warfare as an intrinsic part of their culture. So without further ado, let us take a look at Joshua, one of

God's incredible warriors that pushed forth the 'art of war' as an extension of his social system leaving examples of military principles, both strategic and tactical, as well as leadership and personal conduct.

Grand Strategy To Assemble Warrior

Joshua Invades Canaan

In the area of grand strategy, Joshua the strategist, invaded the land of Canaan from the east in order to stay away from the Via Maris, the modern day name for an ancient trade route, dating from the early Bronze Age, linking Egypt with the northern empires of Syria, Anatolia, and Mesopotamia — the Mediterranean coast of modern-day Egypt, Palestine, Israel, Iran, Iraq, Turkey and Syria in the main north-south trade route along the Mediterranean.

Joshua's Plan Conquest

Joshua avoided Egyptian interference with his planned conquest. He established logistics - the detailed coordination of a complex operation involving many people, facilities, or supplies base east of the Jordan River that also protected his rear during the invasion and provided a line of retreat, if necessary. Line of retreat the roads passed over as the army advances are ordinarily the roads taken when the army retires or is driven back. From there he sent out spies to gather intelligence.

The Strategy: Invade Canaan

Joshua drove straight into the middle of that narrow country in order to divide it in half. That way he could fight one half, and then turn to face the other half. Joshua strove to take the strategic high ground in the central highlands. By choosing to campaign in the mountains, he favored his troops' fighting abilities, and Joshua negated making effective the chariot strength of his opponents.

Battle Key: Strategic Pursuit

In the tactical area, I will refer to a battle of keys, which involved a southern Canaanite coalition (The Book of Joshua, chapter 10). When Joshua heard this coalition alliance, a political party was besieging an ally,

- Joshua showed decisiveness by quickly going to their rescue.

- Joshua demonstrated mobility by marching all night and thereby gained surprise in the battle the next morning.
- Joshua used the battlefield's geography by attacking from the high ground, and he followed up his initial tactical success by pursuing as relentlessly as he could.
- Joshua then exploited this victory by immediately going onto the strategic offensive in southern Canaan.
- When Joshua subdued that region, he then turned to conquer northern Canaan.

As a tactician, Joshua was careful to observe all religious duties. As a strategist, Joshua appeared to be at a military disadvantage only to divide and conquer.

You tactician, are a strategist, skilled in the art of war. God armed you with the sword, the Word of God, to stand against the enemy's tactics. He equipped you with strength, wisdom, and discernment through His own Spirit to stay strong in the spiritual battle. God invites you to spend time in His Presence, through prayer and worship, pressing in to know Him more. It's in your prayers that you learn God's concepts (His mind), God's theory (His word), God's battle plans (His design) God's action (His movement), and God's policy (His system).

Though the warfare may be physically and psychologically oriented, principles of strategy still apply. *"The weapons we fight with are not the weapons of the world. On the contrary, they have divine power to demolish strongholds".* 2 Corinthians 10:4. However, you are able to formulate strategies. How? Through prayers, worship, and your Intercession. The strategies are given to process to take advantage of God's wisdom to overcome the enemy.

About the Author:

Dr. Lovella Mogere, is an entrepreneur, #1 best-selling author and motivational speaker. She empowers women globally to live life intentionally by tapping into the power of intentional thinking. To learn more about Dr. Mogere visit www.lovellamogere.com.

Waging War

"The Challenge"

Explains the economy of warfare and the successes of decisive engagement This section advises that successful military campaigns require limiting the cost of competition and conflict

SHANAIRE HUNTER

Chapter 2

A Rewarding Journey

Warfare, for a girl who seemed like she could take on the world. A girl who could fight anyone who brought her harm. I feared fighting something I could not visibly see. How do I agree to an assignment that left me up at night scared to sleep? How do I become a warfare intercessor with feelings of uncertainty and not knowing what I am up against? Interacting with deliverance to make myself feel complete or not seem like a punk, although, I wanted nothing to do with it and battling with fear internally. My denial of who I am has not only hindered me but caused confusion in my marriage.

I decided that not only was I going to look like I could take on the world, but I was going to do it. Along with my agreement to do what the Lord asked, I received a fire that burned inside so strong it made pretending a distant act. I was ready for war, ready to be on my post.

I was bringing hell to the enemy and his clones. In the book of Psalms chapter 91:5 it states, "Thou shalt not be afraid for the terror by night; nor for the arrow that flieth by day." That scripture brought me comfort at night while I slept. Although that scripture brought me comfort, being a warfare intercessor meant I had to end my relationship with sleep. I know it sounds crazy, but a lot of times, you will be woken up from your sleep to intercede.

How can two people walk together unless they agree? I have been married for about three years. My husband has always made it clear that he knew he was being called into warfare. During our conversations, I nodded my head as if I agreed but never really committing wholeheartedly. One day I was given the assignment to bring forth a word on a warfare intercessor. I was given the assignment two weeks in advance and ignored it the entire time. On the day of the assignment at 5:30 in the morning, I woke up and began hearing God speak. I wrote the word warfare down, and he gave me the rest of my words.

I stood before everyone and began to admit my truth. I did not want anything to do with warfare. I also told them that I gave my yes to God. I jumped up with a roar in my belly. I was excited as I gave my yes to the Lord. I give you my yes! So, you see how two can't walk together unless they agree.

I submitted to my calling, and the love in my marriage increased. It seemed that most arguments stopped. Now we walk side by side in agreement; things are getting done. Doors are being opened, and lives are being changed. Seeing the freedom in the eyes of those who were bound to bring so much joy to me. See, I only saw this calling as something that stole my sleep, not as something that would help others sleep peacefully. Many are up being tormented by these clones, these bullies. Seeing peace on the face of those who were bound is reward enough.

Are you familiar with that song that says, "Here's my cup Lord I lift it up Lord come and quench the thirsting of my soul"? I sing this song at the top of my lungs, knowing I can only do this with the Lord filling me up. I stopped feeling like this was something I was dragged into, but as something I just needed to be present for. We are vessels giving our will to God to move through us. Fill me up, I sing. I'm only really any good because you are with me. I continue to sing, "God of heaven feed me till I want no more, here's my cup, fill it up and make me whole." The fulfillment of answering his call is a feeling that makes you feel full even when you are hungry.

I remember going to gatherings and always standing on the wall. I never really socialized just observing the room, looking for intuition to give me a reason to leave. Minutes after my feelings of distrust left my mind, I stood on those walls like a soldier. I even left blue stains from my new denim jeans on those walls. That position was everything to me. I felt the safest and the most alert. It's kind of funny, now that as I grow into my calling and I stand on the wall being a watchman, or better yet watchwoman! Anyway, specifics don't matter. The point is

I stood there, in the very spot, and I will remain until I'm called home.

See, you don't just become something. I have always stood up for those who were being attacked or bullied. I offered my bed countless times at night; I didn't plan on sleeping. I have been a night owl for as long as I could remember. My mother told me that at the young age of one, I would stand. Yes, I did a lot of standing. As a standing toddler, I was in a crib purchased by the family I would one day go to war for. I stood in that crib for as long as I could not say a word, just watching over my mother as she slept. Some nights she said my uncle would sneak in the room and take me with him. Other nights she would wake up during my escape from my post/crib and allowed me to climb out. I noticed that some nights I needed to rest, to be rescued myself. On this journey, you must find balance knowing when to work and knowing when to rest.

The nights my mother said no was like training. All those no's lead up to this moment; I learned that even though I could be doing something else, I should stay on my post—it has been a rewarding journey.

About the Author:

Shanaire Hunter is a prayer warrior, intercessor and gate keeper. With her God given wisdom she finds balance in being a mother, wife and ministry partner. Shanaire is a woman of few words but packs a mean punch. This woman of God will do anything to see the lives of others flourish. She is an advocate for the black sheep of the family. Stopping at nothing to show the rare beauty of being an unbothered black sheep.

Instagram: @The_Hunters107

Facebook: @ Shay Hunter

Facebook: @Hunters Ministries

Attack By Fire

"The Use of Weaponry"

The general use of weapons and the specific use of the environment as a weapon. This section examines the targets for attack, the types of environmental attacks, and the appropriate responses to such attacks

TRAVE' HUNTER

Chapter 3

After The Armor

Open your eyes. You are standing on the frontlines, armored up, sword in hand. You can feel the surge of energy bubbling up on the inside of you. This is excitement. You've studied the other soldiers, how they move, the way they carry themselves, and the way they prey on the enemy. You have it down pat. You rush into battle and soon realize that you are in dire straits. You thought you were ready. Covered from head to toe in what Ephesians 6 told you was the full armor of God that would allow you to stand against the enemy's tactics. Yet, you are confused because it seems as if it is not working. I still got in a car accident. I still lost my marriage, my job. I have bills to pay, and I need to take care of my family. God, why, how did this happen?

You were present for battle, but not prepared for it. Putting on the armor does not make us invincible. A soldier gets armored up to fight a war, not to prevent it from happening. A soldier does not show up to fight a war he has not prepared for. There is more to the armor than just putting it on. There is more to this fight than you can see. The weapons of our warfare are not carnal but are mighty through God to the pulling down of strongholds (2 Corinthians 10:4). This kind of armor is unlike any that you've seen a soldier wear. It is not camouflaged to blend in with its surroundings, and it needs nothing extra than the pieces described and the person under it. This armor is not just a uniform. This armor is the weapon. This means you not only have to be prepared for the war, but you have to be prepared for the armor. You cannot be effective if you are not properly equipped.

Ephesians 6:14-17 describes the full armor of God as "the belt of truth buckled around your waist, with the breastplate of righteousness in place, and with your feet fitted with the readiness that comes from the gospel of peace. In addition to all this, take up the shield of faith, with which you can extinguish all the flaming arrows of the evil one. Take the helmet of salvation and the sword of the Spirit, which is the word of God". You have to be faithful for the shield to work. You have to be saved for the helmet to work. You have to have the word in you and study it for your sword to be sharp enough and to be able to carry the sword in your belt—know the truth and live by it. This means that you cannot be carrying more falsehood than manhood. If you have no kind of morals, then how is the breastplate working for you? If you don't understand how the price that Jesus paid paved the path before you, your feet are not ready for this journey. Without all of this, your armor is defective.

"We wrestle not against flesh and blood,but against the rulers, against the authorities, against the powers of this dark world and against the spiritual forces of evil in the heavenly realms. Therefore put on the full armor of God" (Ephesians 6:12-13). David was given armor that did not fit, that did not belong to him, and was not made for the type of warfare he was entering into. What if he said, "Okay, I'm armored up!" and then went and stood in front of the giant to fight? He would've died! There were armies of soldiers already stationed at the battlefield. These were men who had spent time studying and practicing techniques, carrying their swords, and fighting. None of them were standing on the battlefield when David arrived, and none stood with him as he approached Goliath without the armor Saul gave to him. He took off the physical armor and put on the "right" spiritual armor. He defeated Goliath with a slingshot. What if he had listened to the world—"what are you going to do with that stick and those rocks?" "The giant is going to crush you!" The other soldiers may have seemed more equipped and physically stronger, more skilled than David. The giant towered over him. However, in the spirit, David was the true giant, which was evident when Goliath lost his head and lost his life (See 1 Samuel 17).

David's position was a shepherd. David was anointed to be king. David was purposed to defeat Goliath. To the world, shepherds don't become king, and they definitely do not slay giants. Can you believe that David had the skills to do all 3 of these things? He succeeded at all of these things and more. What you do after the armor is mostly determined by who it is that is under the armor. You must ask yourself:

"Who am I?"

"What is my purpose?"

"What skills do I have?"

As the shepherd became the king, we too are becoming. Sometimes we fail to recognize this because we separate our earthly persona from the spiritual one when our physical skills are the pre-application of our spiritual skills, skill-builders. We think that the spirit doesn't comprehend the earth realm, but God is spirit, and He created the earth. Without Him, neither one is in existence.

However, we understand that we are spirit and flesh, and we classify our roles as such:

Spiritual Persona: minister, intercessor, worshiper, usher, prophet, pastor, teacher.

Earthly Persona: worker, parent, spouse, teacher, neighbor

Both Jesus' earthly and spiritual persona was a carpenter. He had the same role but a different purpose. He was a builder, fixer, laid foundations, and held up the plumb line to make sure a structure was centered. He also destroyed the temple and rebuilt it in 3 days. Jesus smooths out the rough sides, sanding us down, and He tests and measures our hearts... His earthly and spiritual persona coincide. He doesn't drop one to do the other or change who He is to be one or the other.

The skills you have are God-given. It is up to you to pray and seek Him for the spiritual application of those skills. There, your purpose lies in wait. The answer is not as vague as we think. I have many skills and thought that I was supposed to figure out which one to focus on. I use to pray, "Which one do you want me to use, Lord?" He gave you the gifts and talents to reach various people, places, and atmospheres. We look for jobs that fit our skills, but we don't do the same for spiritual things. The word says that the kingdom suffers violence, so there are many openings for spiritual jobs out there. You won't always find them in the places you expect or the places you are planted. In that case, you must start it, fire starter. Spiritual architect, your skills are creating, designing, and building. Where's your portfolio? Let's go!

There are gifts and skills that you possess that you must learn how to use, and then allow yourself to learn and grow in them, and with the right mentor. Over time we build up spiritual tone or lose tone. We get bigger or heavier in the spirit, and we also lose weight. Glean from someone else who may share that skill. Surround yourself with others who you want beside you on the battlefield, not those who may get you killed. Do not let lack of knowledge or guidance hinder you from moving forward. If you're an educator, educate the people, not just in the school. Your students are your assignments that school year. You're a good marketer or real estate agent. Why? What are your skills? Your clients and partners are your assignments. The neighborhood you are marketing is also your prayer target. If you are unsure, pray, "God, you've given me these skills, how can I apply them to the kingdom?"

Intercessors target their prayers based on a need that God has shown them. Pray, "God, where is there a need?" "How can I use the skills you've given me to help this need?" Also, be obedient to where He stations you, soldier. "Go here? Okay." Don't talk-back or rebel like Jonah. God is saying, "Yes, those people. Yes, in that place." Even in prison, Paul spread the gospel. Every day, there's a job for you to do. I make it a point to pray, "Lord, help me to fulfill my purpose for this day. Let something I say or do impact, influence, change, or touch someone." Let this be your prayer. Live each day to make an impact, not an appearance. "Whatever you do, work at it with all your heart, as working for the Lord, not for human masters" (Colossians 3:23).

About the Author:

Travé Nicole is a certified life coach from Houston, Tx, who specializes in performance anxiety, stress management, personal development and purposeful planning. She holds a BA in Sociology and Psychology (2012) and a Masters in HPER (2017).

Travé is the author of the book, Day Breakers: Win Your Day Before It Starts. (2020), Licensed to Carry (2019), Dear Daughter (2018), These Words (2015), and has co-authored the book Role of An Intercessor Vol I and II. She has performed at events such as Queens of the Mic at the Houston Improv Shift Christian Lounge, and Houston

Gospel Fest 2019, where she performed her single, Shift This Place (2019). Travé has been a guest host on RhemaGospel Radio show, The Blueprint with Bea Well, Amazing 102.5fm. Inspiration Sundays with The Wordmatician, WLJ's The Weekend Praise Party with Santoria Black, Gospel Grind Internet Radio, UpSocial Live, Our Life TV Show River Author's Showcase, and much more.

Website: travenicole.life

Facebook: travenicole

Instagram: trave.nicole

Youtube: Travé Nicole

Tactical Depositions

“Positioning”

Explains the importance of defending existing positions until a commander can advance from those positions in safety. It teaches warriors the importance of recognizing strategic opportunities and teaches not to create opportunities for the enemy

ALANA BELL

Chapter 4

The Effective Strategy of the Kingdom Tactician

The effectual fervent prayer of the righteous availeth much.
James 5:19

Who is the Kingdom Tactician? The Kingdom Tactician is the intercessor that is anointed and appointed for the utilization of a carefully planned strategy from the throne of God to achieve a specific end. It is God's intent for His will to be done as in heaven upon the earth. God works with the end in mind for the purpose to fulfill the Kingdom's Purpose that has already been made victorious by God before the beginning of time. The tactician is the one who utilizes that purpose to build in the earth what God has revealed. God will and does reveal and deliver unto the Kingdom Tactician those precise tactics, which are the steps taken to carry out the strategy from God. These tactics are the plans delivered by God to His chosen Kingdom Tactician to achieve and be victorious in the goals God has set forth.

The Effectiveness of the Kingdom Tactician

The effectiveness of the Kingdom Tactician is highly dependent upon and solely relied on the obedience of the intercessor to the word of God. Remember, unless there is total oneness with the Spirit of the living God, then God is not required to hear and release what is from heaven upon the earth. That does not mean God will not honor prayers if He chooses. But, there is a risk that some prayers that we need God to answer He may not because we are not fully surrendered to His will, word, and way. The union and oneness between God's spirit and the obedience of the Kingdom Tactician ensure that every word spoken by God in the assignment will invoke the presence of the anointing upon the Kingdom Tactician to effectively be the catalyst for the work of God to be successfully done on earth.

The Graced Posture

The graced posture for the Kingdom Tactician is that of humility as they walk in the anointing God has released upon them. It is by God's grace that you have been assigned a position in the kingdom to accomplish His kingdom purpose in the earth. Your graceful posture is the anointing for which God can operate through you to others by His Spirit, His Power, and His Might.Your grace posture is a yielded posture of mind, body, soul, and spirit. Being one with God in the spirit is the pathway that leads to full revelation and delivery. The graced posture gives the Holy Spirit the door to bring the powerful revelation through the anointing upon the Kingdom Tactician, the vessel in which God Himself has given heavenly authorization to operate and bring what is required from God.

Warfare

As discussed, your effectiveness as a Kingdom Tactician rests on your commitment to God and His word. To be fully devoted to being in God's presence. To be sold out to all that God stands for and has required of you. You are His vessel, and you are His anointed. Even abiding in God your Father remembers, there will always be warfare for the enemy does not want what God has purposed. It is the Kingdom Tactician's strategy to be in sync with the Holy Spirit, for in this, you will be guided through all things that may want to thwart what God desires through you. The Holy Spirit is the carrier of every strategy and every tactic needed to destroy all warfare that may seek to kill, steal, and destroy the plans of God. God has positioned you for the battle, and you shall be victorious in Christ.

The Order of God for the Tactician

In everything, there is an order, especially where God is concerned. Order reflects being in the divine positioning to receive all that the Holy Spirit delivers. For the Kingdom Tactician, this requires understanding the implementation of your instructions from God; it means the yielding of your eyes, ears, and heart.

God's order for the Kingdom Tactician is for your eyes to directly be focused on the assignment God has given specifically to you. You are in the world but not of the world. There will always be issues about this life we live on earth. Still, God wants the order of your eyes to be able to spiritually pierce through the natural way of seeing and see those issues spiritually to discern what He wants you to see from the past, forward to the present and beyond into the future. He has given the Kingdom Tactician the power to bind and loose, deliver, and set free according to your divine kingdom's purpose strategy.

God's order is for the ears of the Kingdom Tactician to ever be close to His mouth. God will continually be speaking to the Kingdom Tactician for you and God are One. His mouth and your mouth will speak the same things God has commanded upon the earth. To reveal, to align, to break down, and to build up. The anointing upon your ears will be in tune with our ever-speaking God to deliver every word God speaks.

God's order is for the heart of the kingdom tactician to be positioned with His heart. God will use your heart to be the implementation of the action of His hands upon the earth. As the authorized power from heaven, you, as the delivery point in which God operates in this season and in seasons to come. Your heart intertwined with the heart of God creates and delivers His divine purpose to the assignment He has called you to as a kingdom tactician.

Your Frequency and Your Ultimate Purpose

Your effectiveness, posture, understanding your operation towards warfare and knowing the order and the authority in which you were divinely purposed and created sets the frequency of God to be clear, precise, and to accomplish all the divine purpose and will of God. Full of purpose, full of authority, full of power, and the promise of victory from the throne of heaven. You are now on point. You are now ready and equipped to establish the kingdom's purpose and promises of God. You are of great influence for the kingdom of God. God wants to move upon His people in such a manner that the people of God are not waiting to experience what God has truly prepared for them in heaven only. Those same people from you as God's appointed anointed Kingdom Tactician are now given a means by which God operates by you like the Kingdom Tactician to bring upon the earth now. God's will for His people is to experience life now in fullness that His people will have true peace, power, authority, and the true ability to worship Him in Spirit and Truth. Your hands, Kingdom Tactician, will hear from heaven, divinely go forth with

God's strategy and create as God is the ultimate Creator, and by His instruction, you will now create and deliver that His will be done in heaven as on earth. You are the pathway to ensure victory for the divine will of God.

Prayer

Heavenly Father, God, we thank You for Who You are. We know God that all who worship You must do so in spirit and in truth. This day God, we thank you for the eyes that see as you see. Eyes that will discern that which is seen by the natural because you have given your kingdom tactician spiritual sight to overtake and overthrow the enemy for we see by your spirit God what must be done through the power and sight we have received of You. God, we thank You for the ears that are in tune with Your mouth as we hear only what You say. We believe and act upon nothing, but Your words unto us, our ears are yielded to You. God, thank You for the clean heart you have delivered unto your Kingdom Tactician so that Your purpose for us connected to your divine will is perfected for we are perfect even as You are perfect by our total submission, mighty God. Thank You, Father, for your Holy Spirit that rests upon each Kingdom Tactician as each of us goes forth in Your will and Your promise of purpose for our lives. Thank you, God, for the Holy Spirit's guidance to accomplish your strategies through the workings of the Kingdom Tactician on earth. Thank you, God, for You being God and anointing and empowering your Kingdom Tactician in all things to attain victory as we walk according to Your will and Your way. In Jesus Name, Amen.

About the Author:

Alana Bell is a pastor, faith-based counselor, and nonprofit CEO. She specializes in grant writing and project management for nonprofits to further organizational capacity. Her skills in administration are her God purposed gifts to further the Kingdom of God.

Contact Info: Facebookbook.com/alana.bell.395

Waging War

“The Challenge”

Explains the economy of warfare and the successes of decisive engagement This section advises that successful military campaigns require limiting the cost of competition and conflict

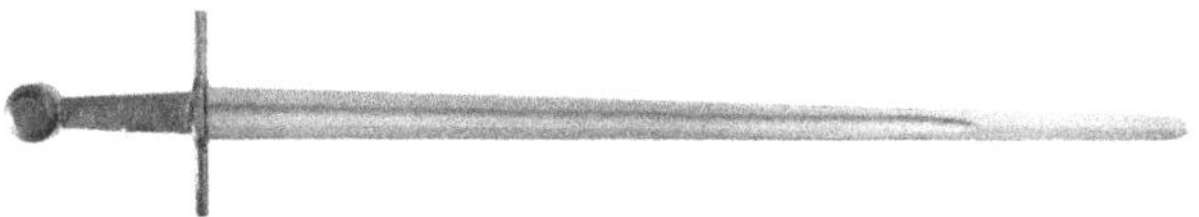

JESSIE BURTS

Chapter 5

Arise To Battle

"For we do not wrestle against flesh and blood, but against principalities, against powers, against rulers of darkness of this age, against spiritual hosts of wickedness in the heavenly places" Ephesians 6:12 NKJV

This scripture tells us that we are in a BATTLE; it informs us of what we are fighting against. When you were born, warfare already existed. "Behold I was brought forth in iniquity and in sin my mother conceived me" (Psalm 51:5 NKJV). From the moment of each man's birth, sin already exists. Are there unseen forces against you? Do attacks persist without any apparent reason against yourself or your family? There are intangible areas in our lives that simply demand a bolder attentive offense in battle.

There was a time raising my children that I desired a larger apartment. The little ones were growing so fast, and we undoubtedly needed more space. Each time I tried to move out of my one-bedroom apartment, it seemed that I could not break free; obstacles formed blockades against my desires. Either the new apartment was taken, or the managerial staff forgot my request. We stayed in that one-bedroom apartment for twelve years; however, during this time, God began to teach me how to pray, and how to target His word specifically concerning our many trials and problematic circumstances. The Holy Spirit would then formulate these strategies in order to counter-attack the enemy. It is in these times that I've learned of warfare within the Kingdom of God. I learned how to break the chains of spiritual bondage, some of which I created in sin, and others derived from generational curses within my family tree.

I was now in the army of the Lord and was to persevere for my children, in refusal of enduring further attacks from my sins or the sins from past generations. It is important to note that I had to change my way of thinking, repent of my sins, and follow Jesus Christ. If this is you, repent and return to Christ. Come back to the battle and stand your ground.

"The Lord is longsuffering and abundant in mercy, forgiving iniquity and transgression; but He by no means clears the guilty, visiting the iniquity of the fathers on the children to the third and fourth generation" (Numbers 14:18 NKJV).

The scripture informs us of unknown wars that exist; generational curses we must oppose. What are generational curses? Generational means the passing down from generation to the next. What is a curse? The word curse means evil powers that befall a person or persons. God chooses whom He desires to do His will, thus raising one up to fight against things we cannot see. As believers, we are called to battle; to fight the good fight of faith. This fight is against spiritual things - things we cannot see with our natural eyes.

To begin our oppositional stance within this fight we must seek God and ask for His Help. Allow the Holy Spirit to speak, train, and teach us how to stand against the enemy. He will grant us specific weapons to combat our adversary. Next, we must be courageous. "Finally my brethren, be strong in the Lord and the power of His might" (Ephesians 6:10 NKJV). Your strength does not come from yourself; you must rely on God and God-alone. God endows us with our weapons, tools, and war clothes. "Put on the whole armour of God, that you may be able to stand against the wiles of the devil" (Ephesians 6:11 NKJV).

Ephesians 6 provides this next strategic step. We must fully dress in the Spirit. "Therefore take up the whole armour of God, that you may be able to withstand in the evil day, and having done all, to stand" (Ephesians 6:13 NKJV). To stand means to remain in an unwavered position. Do not allow the enemy to disposition your feet. When dressing - first, we gird our waists with our belt of truth. This means to speak and stand on God's word; to do this we must know His word (e.g., creating and spending undisturbed time in communion with the Lord). We must allow God's truth to be the final authority. After this, we must put on our breastplate of righteousness, covering ourselves in the hope and faith of God. Our feet also must be covered with the preparation of the gospel of peace. Walking in God's perfect peace means believing and knowing that whatever the enemy throws our way, our Heavenly Father will protect and blanket us under His wings. Next, we take up the shield of faith that quenches all fiery darts of the wicked one. Our helmet of salvation covers our minds in the word of God, as we meditate on His word daily. To complete our attire, we need the sword of the Spirit - which is the word of God. When enemy based thoughts, feelings, and emotions come into our minds, we must remember that "the word of God is living and powerful, and sharper than any two-edged sword, piercing even to the division of soul and spirit, and of joints and marrow, and is a discerner of the thoughts and intents of the heart" (Hebrews 4:12 NKJV).

"Praying always with all prayer and supplication in the spirit, being watchful to this end with all perseverance and supplication for all the saints" (Ephesians 6:18 NKJV).

The Lord gives us a strategy to wage war against the enemy. What does strategy mean? It's defined as coming up with a way or ways to defeat your opponent. This is done through prayer, praise, and worship. Spending time in God's presence and allowing the Holy Spirit to speak to you. Also, by prayer and fasting, please read Isaiah 58.

Warriors, the call is now to arise, put on your armour and join the good fight of faith for those who remain on the wall. Stand your ground and continue to wage war, for you have the victory. If you are new to the battle, I encourage you to be of good cheer, for you are not alone. God has an army that has not bowed down. "Yet I have reserved seven thousand in Israel, all whose knees have not bowed down to Baal, and every mouth that has not kissed him" (1 Kings 19:18 NKJV). Please read the entire chapter at your leisure; God had reserved an army. Elijah was a prophet who ran to hide from Jezebel because she sought to take his life. He had just won a mighty battle for the Lord, yet he ran in fear for His life. Later he was called by God to come out of the cave. Do not hide from the enemy; get back up, arise, and take back your territory. Get back into the rank, come out of hiding. The Lord has need of thee! And as David defeated Goliath in the name of the Lord of Hosts, with a stone, he prayed, and the Lord went before him. Please read 1 Samuel 17. Pray and invite the Lord into your battles.

There are unforeseeable forces in life that demand our attention. Ask yourself what demands yours? Find the scriptures in the word of God that speak against it. Bind and lose the word of God into your situation. “And I will give you the keys to the Kingdom of heaven and whatever you bind on earth will be bound in heaven, and whatever you loose on earth will be loosed in heaven" (Matthew 16:19 NJKV). Use your weapons to pull your family and loved ones out of bondage. Arise and pray for this world and our nation.

Father in Heaven, I thank You, I give You all the praise. I pray Your will be done in the life of Your intercessors and warriors. I pray that You give them divine strategy, in this hour, to combat the wiles of the enemy, who is raging war upon this land. I pray Lord, that You will raise up Your warriors and intercessors. I plead the precious blood of Jesus on all who are reading this book - each chapter. I pray for all the authors and their families that You continue to strengthen us. I pray for those who are returning back to battle for courage and guidance in answering the call. I speak and declare that they now arise in Your newness of power with new plans of attack against the adversary. I speak and declare that new warriors will emerge and take up their armour, in precise strategy. I speak and declare victory over every warrior and every intercessor, in Jesus' name. Warriors arise for your time has now come! In Jesus' name - Amen.

About the Author:

Jessie Burts is a licensed and ordained minister. She is the overseer of the ministry Midwife Sessions - helping birth women into their calling. She is the founder of Bound, Now Free Ministries, and has a passion for winning lost souls. Being a prayer warrior is the calling over her life!

Contact her:Maeproverb@yahoo.com
Sow into her ministry: CashApp: $ Jessie31Burts

Tactical Depositions

"Positioning"

Explores the fundamental factors (the way, seasons, terrain, leadership, and management) and elements that determine the outcomes of military engagements.

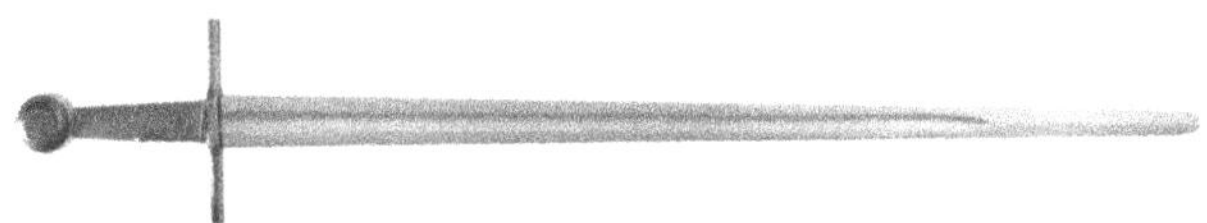

WANDA GENTRY

Chapter 6

The Heart Of An Intercessor

This chapter is about staying true to your call and what the heart of an intercessor should resemble or possess. Before I go into the meat of what I want to talk about, I am going to give you scriptural references that will help support or give validity to my topic and chapter.

First things first, we all know that God is seeking and searching for those whom He can use. Meaning He can trust you to carry out His purpose and plan (will), and not your own personal agenda (will). As Jesus said, "not My will, but Yours, be done (paraphrasing). I left out one word, "nevertheless." Let us put a pin right there because I will come back to that in my closing once I make my point. If we take Jesus as our example because He was and still is our "Chief Intercessor." We can see through his life/example that it was, "All About The Father," and what he wanted and "never" about himself. His desires and wants took a backseat or second place to His Father's Will.

You may be saying, what does all of this have to do with "The Art of War?" Before any man or woman is fit for battle or war, there are some prerequisites (basics, fundamentals, or criteria) that must be met and cannot be taken lightly. What I am talking about can be applied to all areas of ministry.

"You must have a strong/sturdy foundation before you can build and if you want to be successful."

There is no way around it! We must know 1. what to do, 2. how to operate in the realm of the Spirit, 3. who our enemy really is. We know the word of God tells us, "Put on the whole armor of God, ***that you may be able to stand against the wiles of the devil***. If you want more understanding and clarity concerning the armor of God, read Eph. 6: 10-17.

Another thing the word tells us is, ***"For the weapons of our warfare are not carnal but mighty in God."*** (Your weapons are not fleshly or man-made weapons.) They are spiritual.

"You Have To Know The Power Of God You Possess and What You Have Been Called To Do"

You are "Armed and Dangerous!" God has equipped (endowed) you with power. Why? For pulling down strongholds, casting down arguments and every high thing that exalts itself against the knowledge of God.

"It's Hard & Nearly Impossible To Cast Out Something You're Struggling With."

(I know we are not always going to be perfect every day, nor does it mean we won't have issues.) All I can say to you is, as much as possible, we have to stay clean and not bring our struggles into this. This is the part we forget or overlook where it says, "and being ready to punish all disobedience ***when your obedience is fulfilled. (I don't want to take this scripture out of context, but when I read those words this time, they stood out to me.)*** *1. All sin is going to be dealt with; nothing is going to slip by or go unpunished by God. 2. We have a part to play in the salvation and deliverance of others. The word of God* *says in Luke 9:1, "Then He called His twelve disciples together and gave them power and authority over all demons, and to cure diseases." If we continue to read the cannon of scriptures, the next thing you will notice after He gave them power and authority was instructions.* One of the main keys is #1. obedience. Forget about ALL the drama and what I would like to call theatrics, "Just Do What God Told You To Do," and "Keep it Simple Saints" (KISS). Even though you have heard this before, sometimes things are worth repeating again.

Key #2. Make sure you are clean (your hands and your heart is right). The heart of an Intercessor should always consistently stay in a forgiving and repentive state. (Your Posture Matters) We are constantly *laying down* our gifts and our lives on the altar to be crucified in and with Christ. (We operate out of a place of humility and servitude) As Intercessors, we shouldn't be puffed up, we do not exalt ourselves above others, and we shouldn't think of ourselves more highly than we ought to think. As Intercessors, we must wash before we come into the presence of the Lord. We must wash our thought life/wash off the things we may have come in contact with, that was not like God. ***Psalm 24: 3-4 (KJV)***, "3. Who may ascend into the hill of the Lord? 4. He who has clean hands and a pure heart." We must also do a heart check. ***Psalm 51:10***, "Create in me a clean heart, O God, And renew a steadfast spirit within me."

Let me stop here and just talk for a minute. Never think that you have arrived! God may be using you mightily, but remember, "There is another Level and Dimension of God's Grace and His Glory!" If you think that you have arrived, then you are fooling yourself, or the enemy has fooled you. When we do this, not only have we limited ourselves, but our God. In other words, "We Settle," we have found a safe place and have gotten comfortable!

On the other hand, some barely made it out the last time, and now we don't have the energy, passion, or drive to get back in the fight. Don’t allow rejection, being unappreciated, fear or the unknown keep you on the sidelines. You cannot take or operate in another position when you have been called to be on the front line. If you do, you are out of order, out of position, and you will never reach your maximum potential in God.

“Stay In Your Lane So You Can Flow”

I want everyone reading this book to know, "You Are Awesome In Your Own Right." In this dispensational period, I want us to put our focus on the right things.

- An important thing to remember is, "Who you are is not determined by how well you can pray, sing, or prophesy. Who you are is determined by how well you love your neighbor, what you do, and how you live when no one is watching. Can you pray for your enemies, forgive those that despitefully use you, falsely accuse you and say all manner of evil against you?

- Jesus was at ALL points tempted, yet He sinned not! – I know that you are going to be tested as well. There are going to be seasons of testing and trials. God cannot use you mightily if you can't handle or go through anything. Not only do you need to know you can be trusted, but God also needs to know He can trust you! There are numerous seasons we all must go through, such as wilderness seasons and dry seasons. No matter what season you may have to go through, you cannot allow your flesh to get in the way regardless of how long the season may last. We are called to go through for righteousness' sake.

- You must be comfortable as well as confident in who you are. The enemy is going to not only challenge your faith but your identity. There are going to be people who know, respect, and honor who you are and the anointing on your life. You also have to remember not all of them close to Jesus knew who He was when he asked the question, "Who do men say that I am?" Satan tried to get Him not to question his identity but to get Him to prove who he was. More than ever before, it is crucial that we don't believe the lies of the enemy, and we stand against the lies and win!

- Don't allow the enemy to draw you into his tactics or world. We already have too many fleshly, touchy-feely, and emotional Intercessors. These are those who walk by sight; they are up and down and in and out of God. (Sight Creatures/Must See) We know that the just shall "live by faith" (What We Can Not See/We Just Believe). You must develop a trust in God that if He said it, you know that He will perform it!

    - Know that the enemy is going to try to wear you out and wear you down! The weight of the world may feel like it's on your shoulders, you can't find help nor relief from man, and it feels like God is not there (His presence), nor is He listening. This is where the foundation, trust, and relationship you built in/with God comes into play. This is also where if you didn't build it properly, it would be evident not only to you but also to those around you.

"Jesus Went Through Hell To Deliver A People From Hell"

You need to be prepared to go through hell to help save someone else's life. Being an intercessor is not a glamorous thing; it's going to cost you, your family and those around you.

In my Closing.

- You Have Nothing to Prove; Neither Does God - This is a place we All Must get to. There are going to be so many distractions, personal views from others of how they think you should flow, they will also pose the question (in not so many words), "If You Are Anointed" or "If You Have Power" then… Again, I want to remind you to "Stay In Your Own Lane," there are several ways God can use His people to bring forth healing and deliverance. You have nothing to prove. When your anointing and the power of God in you are being questioned, don't you go and put pressure on God to perform on your behalf! He can, and He will, but it's time to take our faith to another dimension. (You must be able to discern between the two of when and when not to.)

- Remember these three: #1. The Cross- "Take up your cross and follow me. #2. The Cup – drink (endure) whatever is in your cup. #3. Temptation – in order to reign with Him, you must suffer with Him. He that endureth temptation shall receive a prize.
- Nevertheless – When Jesus said, nevertheless, it covered everything that you would ever go through, want to complain about, and don't understand. Sickness or disease "nevertheless," lack and poverty, "nevertheless," uncertainty or fear of the unknown "nevertheless." Find the strength in God to push pass "Your IT," and keep it moving. There is a place you must reach called destiny & purpose.

God wants to use you, allow Him to get the glory out of your life!

“Stay True To The Call!”

Pastor Wanda

About the Author:

Wanda serves as an Associate Pastor and Intercessor under the leadership of Senior Pastor, Apostle Dr. Janice F. Thomas and Prophet/ Overseer Bishop Randall K. Thomas of His Kingdom Ministries located in Durham, NC.
Pastor Wanda Gentry is founder of Kingdom Builder International Outreach Ministries and the author of The Enemies of Your Faith.
Wanda's passion is to turn the heart of man back to the heart of God and help others become whole in Christ through teaching the holistic Gospel of Jesus Christ with simplicity, power and demonstration.

Contact Info:
Websitew: www.4everevolving.org

Detail Assessment and Planning

Explores the fundamental factors (the way, seasons, terrain, leadership, and management) the elements that determine the outcomes of military engagements. By thinking, assessing, and comparing these points, a commander can calculate his chances of victory

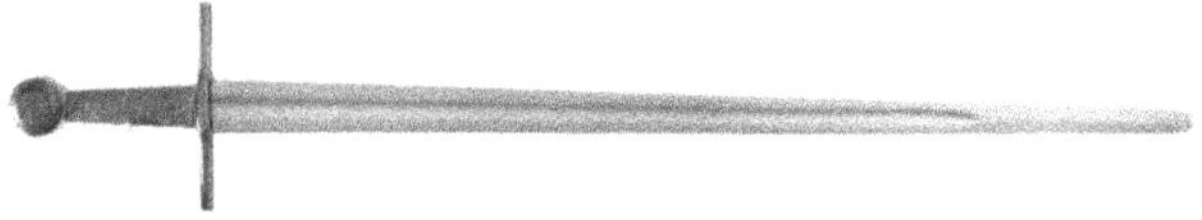

JAMISHA ALFORD

Chapter 7

Preventing A Breach

The one thing that is consistent across all five military branches is their never-ending study of themselves and the opposition they will face. As civilians, we believe that when we prepare for a battle, the focus is solely on the nuances of the enemy and what would cause their failure. We are taught in grade school sporting activities to watch our opponent and study their weaknesses. We become so familiar with our opponent's flaws that we began to manipulate our actions for our team's favor. We are taught in church to know the enemy and his tactics, so we are equipped to stand and fight against them. Rarely are we taught in civilian life to study our own strengths, weaknesses, and areas that need improvement.

Military branches began breaking down the traditional ideologies and egos that serve self in pride, entitlement, and insecurities. They begin the in-depth work of rebuilding each individual into a functioning body of soldiers; one army that moves together, breathes together, and lives together until they are on one accord. Their main goal in finding and strengthening the weakest link is for the entire group to operate as one equally skilled team in order to defeat their enemy. Their main objective in training the soldiers is for them to know themselves as best if not better than they know the enemy. The study of self is almost amiss in civilian life until it becomes critical to our performance. The first self-reflective moment many civilians encounter is at a job interview. The timing of this internal review comes at a disadvantage to many because we do not have the answers readily available. Many people are very skilled at picking out the flaws of others before themselves based on societal norms and how we are taught about the opposition.

The scripture in Matthew 7:3 is a solid indication that this behavior has existed for generations, even the beginning of time. Jesus gives open rebuke to the multitude gathered roundabout, and it is clear that he favors the internal review over hypocritical judgments of others. *He said, "And why beholdest thou the mote that is in thy brother's eye, but considereth not the beam that is in thine own eye*?" God has called us to be a part of his army, and it requires us to be aware of who we are, our purpose, and what role we play in this upcoming war. Let us become impenetrable and stop the enemy from breaching our spiritual borders.

At the forefront of preventing a breach is Leadership. This military position has many titles that coincide with their respective rankings and a strict hierarchy that must be followed. All military leaders must receive what is called "orders" from a higher-ranking authority, sometimes as high as The President of The United States or their country. At this stage, a solid foundation must be created to enable a firm platform for the next ranking to carry out the prevention strategy. Many of us are leaders in our everyday lives without knowing it, even in the absence of certificates, degrees, or ordinations. Those who are parents, the matriarchs and patriarchs of our communities, mentors and many others do the thankless work of guiding multiple generations into phases of life with skills and knowledge that cannot be valued with a price. In our everyday lives, these types of leaders rely on a higher-ranking authority to get wisdom, knowledge, and understanding to deliver the critical and sufficient information to those coming up the ranks behind them. Proverbs 2:6 says clearly, "For the Lord Giveth Wisdom: out of his mouth cometh knowledge and understanding." Allow the Lord to be your Leader and receive a certain and solid foundation, so the gates of hell can never prevail against you.

The next phase of prevention relies on management. In the military, there is a management team responsible for ensuring that business and affairs are running smoothly and completed timely. The manager in our life is Jesus. We must allow him to guide our daily moments and help us complete our required spiritual and natural work timely. We must realize that it all leads back to the spiritual realm and is connected to our purpose in preventing a breach. There is a call for all of us to keep working on our assignments to prevent the devil from devouring our purpose (I Peter 5:8). If the enemy can be successful, he has eliminated a working part of the body of Christ and thus injured the body as a whole. Keeping in mind the idea of an army, everyone involved must be capable and consistent in their part, or else the whole army fails at some point. As written in the word, in John 9:1, Jesus says, " I must work the works of him that sent me, while it is day: the night cometh, when no man can work." Our work can come in the form of natural employment or a spiritual journey in an area of ministry, but the time will come that it must end. Whether your assignment is spiritual or natural, you are a necessary part of the army and are essential to the daily mission of the body of Christ. Allow Jesus to manage your daily walk and work, so when night comes you can hear the highly coveted words of the parable in Matthew 25:21 "Well done, thou good and faithful servant: thou hast been faithful over a few things, I will make thee ruler over many things: enter thou into the joy of thy lord."

The final three phases are all connected and must work simultaneously and in-sync. The way, the season and the terrain are all indicators of how successful or not the plan for prevention will be. The way or route is completely mapped out before battle using maps, GPS, and other intelligence aids. However, the soldiers who are fighting hand-to-hand combat, called "foot soldiers," rely heavily on ancient techniques and instincts to deal with their enemies. What the foot-soldiers know is this "technology fails!" If all of our technology failed today, what would happen to our ability to be trained as soldiers in God's army? Are we equipped with a hand-held bible and commentaries for study? What about a dictionary or thesaurus to look up the words we don't understand? It is time to revisit these ways of studying and integrate them into our routines, so we are equipped for success. As our word has it written in II Timothy 3: 16-17, "All scripture is given by inspiration of God, and is profitable for the doctrine, for reproof, for correction, for instruction in righteousness: that the man of God may be perfect, thoroughly furnished {*equipped – NIV*} unto all good works."

The season of the war will determine the attire, battle weapons, and type of replenishments needed for the army to be sustained during the war. In civilian life, we are taught that the hotter it is, the less clothing we need to keep cool. Contrarily, the opposite is true. Covering up our bodies will keep us cooler and reflect the heat from our actual skin, despite how warm we may feel underneath the clothing. In the military, the clothing covers the body and regulates temperature. It also covers up the battle equipment they may be wearing (guns, knives, grenades, etc.) and protects their body from taking the full hit of an attack from the enemy. The water supply may be increased due to the hot weather in that season of battle and will be rationed out based on the number of soldiers versus the supply. We must learn to gauge the seasons in our life and respond accordingly, despite what may be comfortable for us on a normal basis. This is not a normal time, and we must confront the war with the same abnormality as we are being faced with in our attire, battle weapons, and replenishment.

Lastly, the terrain or the surface in which the battle will take place speaks tremendously to the gravitational advantages of one team to the other. Military branches cover all three areas of battle: land, air, and sea. Similarly, so does our spiritual army. There are demonic spirits that attack the body of Christ on land, through the air, and from the sea. The scripture is bold in boasting that our fight against powers and principalities is a recurring win for God's Army, saying, "And having spoiled principalities and powers, he made a shew of them openly, triumphing over them in it" (Colossians 2:15). As a part of God's Army, we must learn where our terrain is and how to have an advantage in our designated territory.

It's time for battle. Are you ready?

About the Author:

Jamisha is currently the Minister of Music at a local Houston church. She is also a corrections officer for a nearby county and often uses her gifts to assist in setting the atmosphere during worship throughout the week in ministry. She is a mother of one loving and spirited 4-year old boy who is following in the family lineage of music, with hopes of becoming a musician.

Contact Info: Facebookcom/jamisha.alford

Stategic Military Power

“Directing Power”

Explains the use of creativity and timing in building an army's momentum

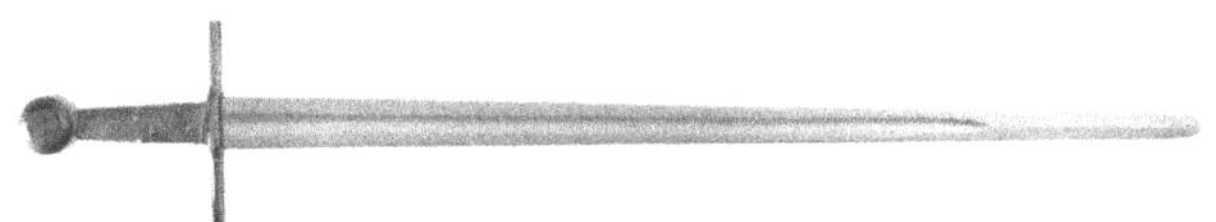

KELLIE HENNINGS

Chapter 8

Engage In Spiritual Warfare

Prayer is where everything begins and ends in the realm of the spirit. As watchmen, we need to ask God to restore our fervor and passion for intercession. Intercession is not a gift or a grace, but it is a privilege to stand in the breaches and keep watch for the deliverance, revival, and restoration for God's people. This is what we were reborn to do.

Are you hungry to see genuine revival hit the nations? Do you want to do the works of Christ? As intercessors, we must first come into agreement with Jesus to be victorious. He is the Chief Intercessor, so we must pattern our prayer lives around Him as the Author and Finisher of our faith. It is vital to have our ears pressed to God's mouth so that our decrees are in total alignment with His will. Then, we should remind of His promises because He honors His word more than His name.

Jesus continually intercedes for us in the church before His father. He invites us to do the same. According to Romans 8:34 and Hebrews 7:25, this ministry of intercession is continuous and unbroken. First, we proclaim God's victory by agreeing with the authority of Jesus. When decreeing and declaring, we must remind God of His promises. Then, we can denounce the enemy by confessing sin, resisting the enemy so he will flee, and renouncing all works of darkness. Engaging in spiritual warfare is primarily done by agreeing with God and disagreeing with the enemy. Intercession is the agreement with what God promises to do and is expressed by declaring His will to get the job done. It is important to mature beyond just denying ourselves, but we die to our thoughts, opinions, and ways of doing things to fulfill heaven's agenda.

Intercessory prayer should be God-centered. The primary strategies should be to unite the body while resisting and breaking up every line demonic opposition. As a general rule, we focus our proclamations directly to God. The New Testament distinguishes between two categories of demonic spirits: those who dwell inside people and those that dwell in heavenly places called principalities, powers, and rulers of darkness. We have the power to rebuke and cast out spirits that reside inside of people. However, we must dismantle principalities in the heavens by directly addressing God.

I have strived to pattern my prayer life after the word of God. I want to be a wholehearted follower of Jesus, conformed into His image (see Romans 8:29.) I lead a lifestyle of intimate intercession like Abraham. I have even left my home, kindred, and country to follow the Lord. Abraham trusted God, and the Lord viewed that as righteousness: “And Abram believed the Lord and the Lord counted him as righteous because of his faith," according to Genesis 15:6. Abraham's trust in God made him an ideal intercessor. We, too, can stand in the gap because we trust in Jesus and His righteousness.

Our motives will never be pure enough, and our

words will always be inadequate, but by the cleansing power of the blood of Jesus, we can stand up and plead for mercy for God's people. I understand the sacrifices of intercession like the widow Prophetess Anna. I value my consecrated existence as I often feel like Daniel, the prophet in exile who prayed three times a day. These are all necessary components of my walk with the Lord. Leviticus 6:13 says, "fire shall be kept burning continually on the altar: and it is not to go out." I pray that you embrace the peculiarity of your assignment in intercession, and God sends those who will add kindling wood to keep your fire burning in weary seasons. We must all find the strategy that works best to remain an effective tool in God's hand.

I would like to share some of the greatest lessons regarding intercession that I learned while battling stage 4 breast cancer. I took on intercession for others who were going through chemotherapy. What you do joyously for another, God will do for you. We must pray from a place of victory and not as though we are working toward it. Our perspective can alter the outcome of our prayers.

As a man thinks in his heart, so is he. We must intercede using specific and intentionally targeted prayers to intercept the plans, plots, traps, and snares of the enemy. I also prayed specifically concerning the blood value levels to keep cancer patients alive. I prayed against side effects to the medications and infections that could complicate the process of healing. It was essential to believe the report of the Lord instead of buying into the doctor's diagnosis. So, whatever the doctor told me concerning my health, I used his report as a tool to teach me how to pray more effectively for myself and others.

The word said, "I shall live and not die and declare

the works of the Lord." After we have done all we know how to do, we must stand on the word of God. It cannot come back void of its intended purpose. The proof is in the pudding. I am still alive four years after a diagnosis of death.

We must operate in a different kind of economy based on Jesus' righteousness. Paul lays it out for us in Romans 4:1-5, "What then shall we say that Abraham, our forefather according to the flesh, discovered in this matter?
[2] If, in fact, Abraham was justified by works, he had something to boast about-but not before God. [3] What does Scripture say? "Abraham believed God, and it was credited to him as righteousness." [4] Now to the one who works, wages are not credited as a gift but as an obligation.
[5]However, to the one who does not work but trusts God who justifies the ungodly, their faith is credited as

righteousness." Our trust and faith, by themselves, do not guarantee success. It is by Jesus' blood and righteousness that we can purchase seasons of mercy. Just ask King Hezekiah how he contended for his life, and God in His mercy granted his request. In intercession, we have the power to defy the odds, see others recover, and live just as he did. God loves it when we lean toward Him in confidence that He hears us when we pray. When we approach Him as a friend and place all our expectations in Him, we permit God to blow our minds! Are you prepared to see God do exceeding and abundantly more than you could ask or think?

About the Author:

Kellie Hennings travels the world fulfilling her passion and purpose of loving people back to life. She is a pastor, entrepreneur, author, certified life coach, and most importantly a worshiper after God's own heart. Apostle Kellie is the Senior Pastor at Impact One International Ministries in Elkhart, In and Nairobi, Kenya.

Contact Info: Facebook.com/kellie.i.hennings

Weak and Strong Points

"Illusion and Reality"

Explains how an army's opportunities come from the openings in the environment caused by the relative weakness of the enemy and how to respond to changes in the fluid battlefield over a given area

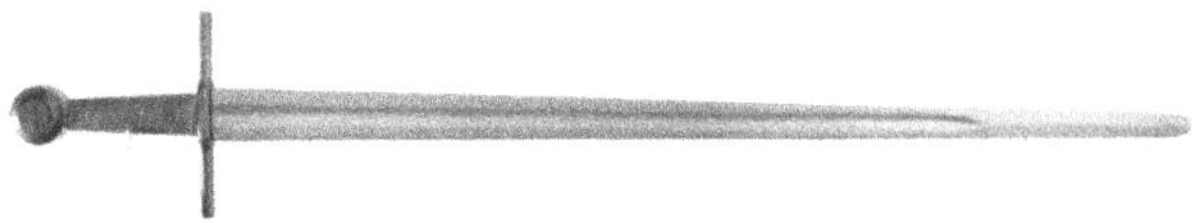

JULIE HITCHENS

Chapter 9

The Rules of Engagement

All armies in the natural world have induction procedures, steps that are required to join the forces. The spiritual army also has induction procedures. These are specific requirements for joining the troops. There is the Importance of Conversion. Conversion is turning from one thing to another. It is a process that involves "change." This change is necessary to enter the kingdom of heaven. "Assuredly, I say to you, unless you are converted and

become as little children, you will by no means enter the kingdom of heaven." Matthew 18:3. Conversion saves us from spiritual death, which is eternal separation from God. Repentance is a must for conversion. Repentance means "to change one's mind." It is a personal and voluntary decision to forsake sin and enter fellowship with God. Repentance that results in conversion is impossible without God's help. That is why God sent His Son, Jesus. Only Jesus can provide the help that is necessary for turning to God. Scripture says that "salvation is not possible through any other person but Jesus," Act 4:12. Conversion and repentance is a must before being enlisted in God's army. According to 2 Corinthians 6:2, today is the day for your salvation. You can receive this beautiful gift through repentance and prayer, confession,
(example below).

Heavenly Father, I come to you in the name of your Son, Jesus Christ. I acknowledge my (wrongs) sins before you. I repent of my sins. I accept Jesus Christ as my Savior and the Lord of my life. Thank you for your provision of salvation for me, in Jesus' name.
Amen.

Jesus said no one could come to Him unless God, the Father, helped him to do so. It is God who draws us to repentance: "No one can come to Me unless the Father who sent Me draws him," John 6:44. The goodness of God is another way that God appeals to people to repent.

Water baptism and the Holy Spirit are also needed. There are over 100 scriptures on baptism. Water baptism symbolizes dying and burying the old you spiritually, and coming up out the water is a declaration of the new life in

Christ spiritually, which means your heart has been changed, and you declare I am spiritually born again. Being baptized in water is a symbol of being purified by God and your sin(s) forgiven. Baptism symbolizes the washing away of our sins.

And Peter said to them, "Repent and be baptized every one of you in the name of Jesus Christ for the forgiveness of your sins, and you will receive the gift of the Holy Spirit," Acts 2:38. So, baptism in the Holy Spirit is a necessity for being in the Kingdom of God and necessary before being enlisted in God's army. Once the Holy Spirit baptizes you, God then brings you into his kingdom, Act 2.

On the day of Pentecost, the Holy Spirit came upon them, and they spoke in foreign languages and were baptized in water (Acts 2: 10-11:18). (Refer to Joel 2:28.)

Just like in the natural, no soldier is sent to battle without first receiving basic training, which prepares him to enter the combat zone or the battlefield.

Rules of Engagement

Just as there are Rules of Engagement in natural war, there are also Rules of Engagement for Spiritual Wars.

Definition:

Rules of engagement (ROE) are the internal rules or directives among military forces (including individuals) that define the circumstances, conditions, degree, and manner in which the use of force or actions might be construed as provocative, may be applied. Knowing the laws of war before entering combat is a necessity, whether it's natural or spiritual.

The Commander is the Holy Spirit, who gives us clear instruction, objective, task, or our assignment. He is also the one who determines our rank and level. There is an order in God's Kingdom, and we are called to do them the Father's way.

It's not just enough to identify our adversary or enemies, but to know or understand his strategy is how we are victorious in a waged war. In the natural all soldiers go to training which is called boot camp, well also the spiritual soldiers of The Kingdom of God must be a trained disciple to be effective. We see Jesus, our Lord, prepare his students for three and a half years before releasing them into the battlefield. Yet there was still causality of war. When the art of war is not fully understood, there will be casualties. We must first understand the natural and spiritual worlds.

Man exists in two worlds, the natural world, and the

spiritual world. The natural world is that which can be seen, felt, touched, heard, or tasted. It is considered a tangible and visible world (Earth). The country, nation, city, or place where you live is part of the natural world. We are a resident in a natural kingdom located on one of the visible continents of the world. There is another world in which you live. That world is a spiritual world. You cannot see it with your physical eyes or touch it, but it is just as real as the natural world you live in.

Paul speaks of this division of natural and spiritual. There is a natural body, and there is a spiritual body. (I Corinthians 15:40). Two Kingdoms, the Natural Kingdom that all men live in, and the Spiritual Kingdom, which we exist in. There is a battleground of war all around man that is invisible to the natural eyes. Yet the Spirit realm or Spirit world is more real or realistic than the natural world because it is God’s world. Yet for those who are filled with and lead by the Holy Spirit, God has given us authority over the natural world and those spirits which enter the natural world that oppose God's purpose.

Luke 10:15-20, "And thou, Capernaum, which art exalted to heaven, shalt be thrust down to hell. He that heareth you heareth me; and he that despiseth you despiseth me; and he that despiseth me despiseth him that sent me. And the seventy returned again with joy, saying, Lord, even the devils are subject unto us through thy name. And he said unto them, I beheld Satan as lightning fell from heaven. Behold, I give unto you power to tread on serpents and scorpions, and over all the power of the enemy: and nothing shall by any means hurt you. Notwithstanding in this rejoice not, that the spirits are subject unto you; but rather rejoice, because your names are written in heaven."

Rules of Engagement

2 Corinthians 2:11, "Lest Satan, should get an advantage of us: for we are not ignorant of his devices," 2John 2:15-17. "Love not the world, neither the things that are in the world. If any man loves the world, the love of the Father is not in him. For all that is in the world, the lust of the flesh, and the lust of the eyes, and the pride of life, is not of the Father, but is of the world. And the world passeth away, and the lust thereof: but he that doeth the will of God abideth forever."

Before we can do battle with any enemies outside of ourselves, we must first defeat the enemy within ourselves. We must live a God-fearing life daily, sanctified, holy in humility. We should walk in love, live a repented life in total obedience to the Lord. We must forgive those who offend us every day that the enemy can find none of him in you.

Ephesians 6:10-18, "Finally, my brethren, be strong in the Lord, and in the power of his might. Put on the whole armour of God, that ye may be able to stand against the wiles of the devil. For we wrestle not against flesh and blood, but against principalities, against powers, against the rulers of the darkness of this world, against spiritual wickedness in high places. Wherefore take unto you the whole armour of God, that ye may be able to withstand in the evil day, and having done all, to stand. Stand therefore, having your loins girt about with truth, and having on the breastplate of righteousness; And your feet shod with the preparation of the gospel of peace; Above all, taking the shield of faith, wherewith ye shall be able to quench all the fiery darts of the wicked. And take the helmet of salvation, and the sword of the Spirit, which is the word of God: Praying always with all prayer and supplication in the Spirit, and watching thereunto with all perseverance and supplication for all saints;"

Understanding spiritual warfare is multi-dimensional; it is impossible to war effectively without the Holy Spirit, revealing strategies and tactics. The Holy Spirit knows the strategies of Satan, and He intercedes for believers engaged in battle: (Romans 8:26-27) (Acts 1:8).

Don't give place to devils and lay aside affairs of the world. The art of war is to know what weapons you have and when and how to use them. We have been given the most lethal weapon in the natural world and the spirit world, that is THE WORD OF GOD, and training is vital to know when to use them defensively or offensively. And when we have done all to stand against the enemy, continue to stand your whole ground.

"Blessed be the Lord my strength which teacheth my hands to war and my fingers to fight." Psalm 144.

About the Author:

Ambassador Dr. Julie Hitchens is an acclaimed Teacher, Apostle/Prophetess, and Psalmist with more than thirty years in ministry. She is also an author and has written eight books to date. She is also an independent gospel recording artist and songwriter.

Ambassador Dr. Julie Hitchens' very existence is to bring the good news of Jesus to people of every color and culture all over the world, literally changing lives one person at a time. Dr. Julie is not afraid to deal with hard relevant issues as it is her passion to fulfill God's mandate for these turbulent times. Her thrust on character building by merging spirituality with everyday living provokes those she encounters to pursue a life of integrity and love.

Contact Info: Facebook.com/jhitchensministries

Tactical Depositions

"The Positioning"

Explores the fundamental factors (the way, seasons, terrain, leadership, and management) and elements that determine the outcomes of military engagements.

DR. VARENDA WILLIAMS

Chapter 10

It's About to Go Down!!!

One day, one of my co-workers called me after work. After all, I had a workshop to attend, so I politely asked her to periodically check on my classes even though I had a highly capable substitute teacher in my classroom. My co-worker's voice was full of fatigue and frustration. *"MS. WILLIAMS!!"* she screamed. *"The sub said that all of your classes were great. There have been no problems whatsoever. On the other hand, four fights broke out on the*

second floor today. One fight took place on the top stairwell. Another took place on the back stairwell on the west end, and the remaining two fights took place on our end of the hallway."

"Ohhh boy!!" I replied as I let out a deep sigh while shaking my head.

"Ms. Williams, the hallways, looked like a war zone! You know, we don't break up fights. No ma'am!! I didn't sign up for this when I decided to teach! The program didn't prepare us on how to handle this!!"

Of course, educators are strongly admonished not to interfere and stop physical altercations on campus when they occur. However, we can be prepared and equipped for the educational, spiritual war zone regardless of the location from a warfare perspective. If you are wondering how that is possible, just keep reading.

There's this famous cool guy in scripture who was very knowledgeable and proficient while engaging and winning in warfare with absolutely NO military experience or matriculation from any Armed Forces academies. Let's see if you can guess who I am talking about.

He started as a singing shepherd whose sonneteer abilities continue to be read, taught, quoted, and sung by countless others throughout generations. It does not stop there. He was a masterful maestro whose music served eviction papers to evil spirits that occupied any atmosphere. He was a willing worshipper whose avowed demonstration of transparency, love, and raw relationship with God can be seen, felt, and relatable within the scripture pages. He was a witty warrior with numerous victories using the most unconventional and unorthodox weapons, tools, and strategies. Though he received no Purple Heart, God called him a man after His own heart.

You guessed correctly. I'm talking about David. Okay, I get it! You may not be a king, a psalmist, or a musician, BUT you are a worshipper AND a warrior! Just like David, you, too, can be successful in the mechanics and dynamics of warfare. So, how did he do it? What made him so competent, effective, and triumphant?

Let's get one crucial thing understood right from the start. When it comes to warfare, we notice how David consistently went to God for counsel and direction.

"Therefore, ***David inquired of the Lord****, saying, "Shall I go and attack these Philistines?" And the Lord said to David, "Go and attack the Philistines, and save Keilah." (I*

Samuel 23: 2 NKJV)

*"Then **David inquired of the Lord once again**. And the Lord answered him and said, "Arise, go down to Keilah. For I will deliver the Philistines into your hand." (I Samuel 23:4 NKJV)*

So, we see the importance and necessity of seeking, inquiring, and listening to our Commander-in-Chief, the Lord God Almighty, for precision, accuracy, and specifications in warfare engagement.

*"He **<u>teaches</u>** my hands to make war,*
So that my arms can bend a bow of bronze." (Psalms 18:34 NKJV)

"Blessed be the Lord my Rock,
*Who **trains** my hands for war,*

And my fingers for battle" (Psalms 144:1 NKJV)

For one to be taught or trained, one must be teachable. Just because one possesses the essential skills to fight does not necessarily mean that they know and understand warfare logistics or how to implement methods to win. Just because a specific strategy was effective and productive in the previous battle does not guarantee victorious results in an upcoming battle. Just because a kind of weapon was utilized the last time does not mean it is going to be used this time during warfare.

Let us go back to the scripture references in Psalms previously mentioned. Here are two probing questions for thoughtful consideration:

a) So, what does the Lord specifically teach us to do in

times of war and battle?

b) What strategies are our fingers and hands assigned to do to ensure victory over our enemies?

Part one of "The Role of an Intercessor," various purposes, positions, and functions of an intercessor, was identified, as well as the criteria of a marketplace intercessor within the education field. Now, it is time to specify the strategies needed to execute for ultimate conquest and triumph. Let us take a close look at a strategy depicted in Scripture for further deconstruction, operation, and practice:

"See, I have appointed you this day over the nations and over the kingdoms,

To uproot and break down,

To destroy and to overthrow,

To build and to plant. *" (Jeremiah 1:10 AMP)*

Strategic Point #1- To uproot and to break down

When something is uprooted, it is permanently removed. Therefore, it can no longer take up space and energy. After it is uprooted, then the breakdown occurs. The breakdown leads to a total irretrievable decay and decomposition.

Strategic Point #2- To destroy and to overthrow

If an issue is destroyed, that means it can no longer continue to exist, flourish, and multiply. It is annihilated, extinguished, and irrevocable. Overthrow in warfare brings invalidation, confusion, and defeat.

Strategic Point #3- To build and to plant

To build requires establishment and innovation of what is

necessary and vital to be stable and influential. To plant demands inauguration, pioneering, and launching of something new to operate and function to full capacity in the earth.

So, educational marketplace intercessors, you have the strategies and the Word of God!

You are dressed, armed, and fully equipped for battle!

Let's GO!!

Let's OVERTAKE and DOMINATE!!

Let's SYNCHRONIZE and MOBILIZE!

Let's advance UPWARD and ONWARD!!

Let's ASCEND and CONTEND!!

Let's **UPROOT** the labels and statistics that have been placed on our children and the students we teach!

Let's **BREAK DOWN** and pull down every evil report and word curse spoken and written against the students we teach and our own children!

Let's **DESTROY** the lie that our students and our own children can't learn and won't succeed!

Let's **OVERTHROW** the actions of unfair treatment and bullying in our students' lives and our own children!

Let's **BUILD** a fresh foundation that exhibits a productive, healthy learning climate based on the Word of God!

Let's **PLANT** new seeds of scriptural decrees and declarations of divine imagination, intelligence, and creativity that will yield jaw-dropping and record-breaking successes inside and beyond the classroom for our future generation!

Just remember …

You are UNBREAKABLE, UNCHANGEABLE, UNSHAKABLE, and UNSTOPPABLE!

You are FEARLESS, FAITHFUL, and FOCUSED!

You are warriors who WORSHIP and WIN EVERYTIME!!

You are spiritually MOBILE and AGILE……and ready for this HOSTILE TAKEOVER!!

It's ABOUT TO GO DOWN!!!

*"Caleb interrupted, called for silence before Moses and said, "Let's **GO UP** and **TAKE** the land—**NOW**. **WE CAN DO IT**." (Numbers 13:30 MSG)*

About the Author:

Dr. Varenda S. Williams is an ordained preacher, teacher, conference speaker, and dynamic woman that God is using to encourage, train, and instruct the Body of Christ. Dr. Varenda S. Williams has nearly twenty years of experience in the field of education and thirty years in ministry who currently resides in Houston, Texas. Learn more about

Varenda: Email: drladyprof@gmail.com
Facebook: Varenda Williams' Author Page
Instagram: @drvswilliams @varendawilliamsauthor
Twitter: @drvswilliams @VWilliamsauthor

Attack By Fire

The Use of Weaponry

Explores the fundamental factors (the way, seasons, terrain, leadership, and management) and elements that determine the outcomes of military engagements.

YELEINA MORGAN

Chapter 11

Warrior's Arsenal

"For though we walk in the flesh, we do not war after the flesh: For the weapons of our warfare are not carnal, but mighty through God to the pulling down of strongholds; Casting down imaginations, and every high thing that exalteth itself against the knowledge of God, and bringing into captivity every thought to the obedience of Christ; And having in a readiness to revenge all disobedience, when your obedience is fulfilled." 2 Corinthians 10:3-6

Since the enemy's fall, there has been a battle against the fulfillment of God's plan and purpose upon the earth. And as a result, warfare in the spirit is linked to the purpose of God. The enemy battles to bring the heart, mind, spirit, and soul into allegiance to him instead of to Christ. Spiritual warfare is a reality of the believer's daily life, which means that there is always some form of spiritual warfare afoot, and we as warriors are assigned to challenge "principalities, against powers, against the rulers of the darkness of this world, against spiritual wickedness in high places." And we must be prepared to go into, or to join, the battle that the enemy is continuously waging against God's Kingdom and citizens.

As in any natural war, there is a need for trained and skilled warriors. All warriors, whether in the natural or spiritual, have a few things in common; they are disciplined, both internally and externally. They have developed sharp mental focus and are persistent in bringing about a good result. Many different scriptural strategies are implemented in spiritual warfare. The initial battle strategy can be understood when the warrior can identify the enemy before entering the battlefield; study the enemy, his nature, and strategies, and most importantly, a Kingdom warrior must understand and analyze how Jesus dealt with the enemy.

When we look at Jesus Christ in Revelation 19:11-16, we see Jesus fully as a warrior prepared for battle;

"And I saw Heaven opened, and behold a white horse; and He that sat upon him was called Faithful and True, and in righteousness He doth judge and make war. His eyes were as a flame of fire, and on His head were many crowns; and He had a name written, that no man knew, but He Himself. And He was clothed with a vesture dipped in blood: and His name is called The Word of God. And the armies which were in Heaven followed Him upon white horses, clothed in fine linen, white and clean. And out of His mouth goeth a sharp sword, that with it He should smite the nations: and He shall rule them with a rod of iron: and He treadeth the winepress of the fierceness and wrath of Almighty God. And He hath on his vesture and on His thigh a name written, King Of Kings, And Lord Of Lords."

Jesus Christ has reclaimed dominion over the world, the enemy, and his forces. But the kingdom of darkness continues to wage war throughout the world. The enemy plans to take possession of territory and influence men and women to act in manners contrary to the will and plan of

God. As warriors, we realize that this battle will continue until the final encounter.

While Ephesians 6:14-17 reveals to us how we are to be dressed appropriately or geared up to go into battle, the armor of God gives us the power to stand against the wiles of the enemy. While this is the military uniform that every believer should be clothed in, other weapons must be a part of every warrior's arsenal as they seek to defend the Kingdom and every Kingdom citizen. The Greek word for weapons is hoplon. It means "any tool or implement for preparing a thing; arms used in warfare, weapons; an instrument." [1] The Greek word for warfare is strateia, which is defined as "an expedition, campaign, military service, warfare." [2]

The fundamentals of a warrior's battle plan for spiritual

warfare is based on six major points:

The Word of God:

To rightly apply the Word of God in spiritual warfare, you must know the Word of God as directed in 2 Timothy 2:15, where we read "Study to shew thyself approved unto God, a workman that needeth not to be ashamed, rightly dividing the word of truth." We must study, meditate, and memorize it, for failure to do so opens opportunities for the enemy to gain ground and possibly cause one to lose the upper hand. "The god of this age has blinded the minds of the unbelievers, to keep them from seeing the light of the gospel of the glory of Christ" (2 Corinthians 4:4).

Power and Authority:

Another part of the warriors' weaponry and battle strategy is in rightly assuming power and authority over the enemy. Jesus appointed this authority to His followers: "Then He called His twelve disciples together and gave them power and authority over all devils, and to cure diseases." (Luke 9:1) However, we must be mindful and remember that authority and power are two different things. Authority comes through Jesus Christ and power by the Holy Spirit.

Prayer:

Prayer is our most effective and powerful weapon in any warrior's arsenal. It is something that the enemy does not have, that the enemy cannot stop, that the enemy cannot impede or obstruct. There is no defense for this type of weapon. Prayer is warfare activity; it is the call sent out to the Lord of hosts for support and intervention.

Fasting:

Fasting, combined with prayer, is another weapon

available to wage active warfare. Fasting does not change God, but it changes you. In Matthew 17:21, Jesus said that "However, this kind does not go out except by prayer and fasting." Fasting applies pressure to the spiritual realm, and sometimes it is necessary to maintain that pressure before there is a breakthrough.

Keys of The Kingdom:

Jesus gave all believers the keys of the Kingdom, including the power to bind and loose. Matthew 16:19 teaches, "And I will give unto thee the keys of the Kingdom of Heaven; and whatsoever thou shalt bind on earth shall be bound in Heaven; and whatsoever thou shalt loose on earth shall be loosed in Heaven." The principle of binding and loosing is a vital strategy in overcoming the power of the enemy. When one recognizes what to bind to loose and then act upon this wisdom, the enemy will be defeated.

The Name of Jesus:

One of the weapons in a warrior's arsenal that requires wisdom and revelation to wield it properly is found in the power of the name of Jesus Christ. Throughout the Scriptures, we are given insight as to the power of the name of the Lord:

Jeremiah 16:21 "Therefore, behold, I will once cause them to know, I will cause them to know mine hand and my might; and they shall know that my name is The LORD."

John 14:14 "If ye shall ask anything in my name, I will do it."

John 16:23 "Verily, verily, I say unto you, Whatsoever ye shall ask the Father in my name, He will give it to you."

We have been called to fulfill the Great Commission, and as warriors, we are instructed in Mark 16:17, have been commissioned to, "cast out devils; they shall speak with new tongues; They shall take up serpents; and if they drink any deadly thing, it shall not hurt them; they shall lay hands on the sick, and they shall recover." Also, to overcome every power of the enemy through the name of Jesus, which is more powerful than any other name. Scripture declares in Ephesians 1:21 that the name of Jesus is, "Far above all principality, and power, and might, and dominion, and every name that is named, not only in this world, but also in that which is to come."

Any combat training and tactical maneuver requires one to go through a process of preparation to be skillfully adept in the use of every weapon found in their arsenal. This process includes understanding the tactics and strategies necessary on the battlefield, gathering intelligence, analyzing the enemy's level of warfare, recognizing the enemy's intention, and knowing the territory upon which the battle will be fought. Strategy and tactics are critical in warfare. Strategy, from Greek equivalent to the modern word "strategy," would have been "strategike episteme" or (general's knowledge) "strategon sophia" (general's wisdom).[3] is the plan or set of goals and tactics are the actions or steps taken to accomplish your strategy. Strategies are useless steps, when (not or) tactical measures aren't implemented to achieve it. The word "tactic" comes from the Ancient Greek "taktikos," which loosely translates to "the art of ordering or arranging." [4]

Now, once the weapons necessary have been amassed, and receive strategies from the Holy Spirit, then and only then can we effectively engage the enemy. Any warrior fighting in battle without these weapons would be equivalent to going to war empty-handed. "How can one enter into a strong man's house, and spoil his goods, except he first bind the strong man?" Matthew 12:29 and the failure to properly be trained and equipped can result in engaging in a battle using outdated and non-effective weapons used previously in a past season. In other words, while the goal remains the same, to destroy the kingdom of darkness and all attempts to overthrow God's Kingdom, the steps and tactics we take must be adaptable and adjustable. There are standard strategies and weapons that we must always employ and deploy, but to be victorious in warfare, one needs to have and to use the right weapon.

Spiritual warfare is a multidimensional effort in which the spiritual realm coexists in parallel to and concordance with our world. With that in mind, it is imperative that warriors before entering into battle with an enemy, equip and armor themselves for combat by learning to engage their enemies using different combat tactics and weapons available in their arsenal to maximize their effectiveness. 1 Peter 5:8 teaches us to "Be sober, be vigilant; because your adversary, the devil, as a roaring lion, walketh about, seeking whom he may devour." However, there is no guarantee that the same weapon used in previous battles will bring the same results now, thus rendering you ineffective and exposed to retaliation.

Every well-trained warrior has an arsenal of spiritual weapons at his or her disposal and should have full working knowledge and understanding of these weapons and how to wield them properly. Weapons such as prayer, decreeing, and declaring the Word of God, revelation, keen understanding of God's timing, and an authentic relationship with God are imperative to any warrior's arsenal. Spiritual warriors must see situations and people as

God sees them and be strategic in how we approach them. First, we define our goal; if we don't know our goal, we won't know how to attack. The goal should be well-defined, specific, and comprehensive; if it's vague, indefinite, or incomplete, the warrior will fall short of their purpose. So, when you can see the layout of God's plan, the weapons used by His warrior will take on potency and intensity to dismantle and uproot demonic forces, reclaiming territory under siege by an enemy stronghold.

Decreeing and declaring activates the creative power within us because we have been created in God's image and likeness. For us to walk at this level of authority and power, we must be carefully trained and walk in complete agreement with God.

In 2 Kings 6, we see an authentic relationship with

God as another weapon when Elisha's close relationship with God made him privy to the enemy's plans when he was allowed to hear the king's private words in his spirit. Spiritual warriors see beyond the natural into a realm of the Spirit where God lives. Strategic implementation of a warrior's weapons targets the enemy's powers and principalities. While our tactical weapons focus on the enemy powers and principalities, warriors must be keen and understanding of circumstances in both natural and spiritual realms and employ Spiritual mapping, which is the identification and definition of a geographical territory under oppression to map the influence of enemy infiltration over nations and people.

Warriors must be able to discern and understand chronological time, as well as spiritual and political time. "And of the children of Issachar, which were men that had understanding of the times, to know what Israel ought to do; the heads of them were two hundred; and all their brethren were at their commandment." 1 Chronicles 12:32

Warriors are a different breed in that they carry themselves differently than most, and when they move or speak, they do so with purpose and intent. Kingdom warriors know who they are and what they are capable of, but just as in natural warfare, any unused weapons that do not inflict casualties on the enemy will not win wars. Your spiritual weapons are affected by your will to use them. God entrusts us with weapons to go into battle, but it is our responsibility to utilize them to stir divine intervention from Heaven.

Arise, Warriors!

You have been recruited and commissioned to

serve in an elite strategic and tactical unit of God's Kingdom. Your decrees and declaration; your prayers imbued with divine power and authority; your fasting to receive Kingdom keys and the name of Jesus are part of your arsenal of weapons. They are given to defeat, cast down, destroy and dismantle every illegal advancement by the enemy of your soul. Understand that the demands and expectations are high, but know that your faith, obedience, and with all of Heaven backing you, you are already victorious for "There is no one like the God of Israel. He rides across the heavens to help you, across the skies in majestic splendor." Deuteronomy 33:26. You are warriors! You have been armed with spiritual weapons, specific and precise, to overcome all the evil plans of the enemy. Take your place, change the atmosphere around you, make accurate decisions of strategic and tactical impact that disrupt and incapacitate every maneuver of the enemy. The gates of darkness shall tremble at your presence, the Word of God as your sword unsheathed resounds across the land claiming and reclaiming souls and territories as you establish on earth that which is in Heaven through the grace and gifts God Has given to you as His mighty warrior.

About the Author:

Yeleina Morgan, a native New Yorker, a graduate of Regent University with an Associate Degree in Biblical Studies is a published author of "From Spiritual Disability to Spiritual Maturity" and a Co-author of The Role of An Intercessor. Yeleina is a catalyst who ignites and motivates others to achieve their dreams.

Contact Info: Facebook.com/yeleinamorgan716

References

[1] G3696 - hoplon - Strong's Greek Lexicon (KJV). (2020). Retrieved from https://www.blueletterbible.org/lang/lexicon/lexicon.cfm?Strongs=G3696&t=KJV

[2] G1 - alpha - Strong's Greek Lexicon (KJV). Retrieved from https://www.blueletterbible.org/lang/lexicon/lexicon.cfm?Strongs=G4752&t=KJV

[3] Horwath, R. (2006). The Origin of Strategy. https://www.strategyskills.com/Articles_Samples/origin_strategy.pdf

[4] Horwath, R. (2006). The Origin of Strategy. https://www.strategyskills.com/Articles_Samples/origin_strategy.pdf

Attack By Stratagem

"Plan Attack"

Explores the fundamental factors (the way, seasons, terrain, leadership, and management) and elements that determine the outcomes of military engagements.

SHENEKI WHITE

Chapter 12

Attack By Stratagem

Isaiah 53:4-5 NLT "*Yet it was our weaknesses he carried; it was our sorrows that weighed him down. And we thought his troubles were a punishment from God, a punishment for his own sins! But he was pierced for our rebellion, crushed for our sins. He was beaten so we could be whole. He was whipped so we could be healed.*"

What is stratagem?

A stratagem is any clever scheme- i.e., a carefully worked out plan of action.

God's stratagem:

To send His one and only Son to die on the cross to save humankind from our sinful nature.

2 Corinthians 5:21 NLT, "*For God made Christ, who never sinned, to be the offering for our sin so that we could be made right with God through Christ."*

Why doesn't God simply forgive us? Why must He die for us? Because God is Holy, and He must judge sin. Would a judge let a criminal found guilty go unpunished? At the cross, God poured out His judgment on His Son, making it possible for Him to forgive us. That was God's carefully worked-out plan of action.

Our battles are our sins: hatred, greed, lust, pride, the ungodly ways of the world, physical ailments, misdealings with people, and death, just to name a few.

Ephesians 6:10-12 NLT "*Be strong in the Lord and in his mighty power. Put on all of God's armor so that you will be able to stand firm against all strategies of the devil. For we are not fighting against flesh-and-blood enemies, but against evil rulers and authorities of the unseen world, against mighty powers in this dark world, and against evil spirits in the heavenly places.*"

We are caught in the conformation of not fighting against flesh and blood. We may think our struggle is against people who get in our way, but that is not so. The reality is that we are in a spiritual battle that can only be fought with spiritual weapons. While it is unhealthy to deny the devil and demons, it would be in vain to deny their existence. The weakest believer has enough of the power of God, under His authority, to cast out every demon, without fear.

Ask yourself, so what are we up against?

The devil's stratagems. His warfare is crafty and premeditated. The devil seeks out to entrap believers, often disguising himself as an angel of light. 2Corinthians 11:14. Our stratagem of protection; put on the full armor of God. Ephesians 6:13 NLT *"Therefore, put on every piece of God's armor so you will be able to resist the enemy in the time of evil. Then after the battle you are still standing firm."*

What is the full armor? I am glad you asked.

Ephesians 6:14-17 NLT "*Stand your ground, putting on the belt of truth and the body armor of God's righteousness. For shoes, put on the peace that comes from the Good News so that you will be fully prepared. In addition to all of these, hold up the shield of faith to stop the fiery arrows of the devil. Put on salvation as your helmet, and take the sword of the Spirit, which is the word of God.*"

Under all physical manifestations of any struggle, there is a spiritual reality. If you have a problem with another person, it is not a matter of the flesh; it's a spiritual problem.

All struggles and darkness have one source, and

that's the devil. I mentioned earlier that the devil has one target, and that is to entrap believers.

Our battles are spiritual. The spiritual weapons of prayer, godliness, and the truth is revealed by the Holy Spirit, and the Word of God is our only defense. Our attack of stratagem.

The Bible is about a Kingdom, and Jesus Christ is our King! He came to earth to bring His kingdom. God had a plan of action to keep humans in the world, but also, and most importantly, to keep us from the evil in it. Our history is sin. Sin has a drug-like quality. We always want more and more because it seems satisfying. Once we no longer receive the same satisfaction as we got the first time, we continue to chase sin. We become slaves to sin, and in the process, our heart hardens. Once we think of sowing a sinful act, we should not act upon it. Once a thought becomes a habit, that habit becomes a necessity. Our will is the power by which the mind makes choices and acts to carry out those choices. Lord, we pray-Not our will, but Your will be done in our lives.

God's stratagem:

He created the earth to expand His territory so we can have power over the earth. He created humans in His image so that we can be like Him.

We cannot run earth in our strength, nor can we defeat our spiritual battles with our flesh. God sent His Son to live amongst us to feel what we feel and experience what we experience. He became a human being.

Why would He do this?

To reveal Himself to humanity, to fulfill God's promises, bring salvation, and destroy the works of the devil. And to prepare the way for our heavenly destiny. God's plan of action is set up for our life, deliverance, joy, and salvation.

2 Corinthians 5:17, 21 NLT "*This means that anyone who belongs to Christ has become a new person. The old life is gone; a new life has begun! For God made Christ, who never sinned, to be the offering for our sin, so that we could be made right with God through Christ.*"

God's stratagem:

To enter the human battlefield. This was accomplished with God becoming a human being. Christ coming was to die on the cross for the sins of the world. He died in our place so that we do not have to suffer eternally.

2 Corinthians 5:19, 21 NLT "*For God was in Christ, reconciling the world to himself, no longer counting people's sins against them. And he gave us this wonderful message of reconciliation. For God made Christ, who never sinned, to be the offering for our sin, so that we could be made right with God through Christ.*"

Stratagem: Intercession -The act of intervening on behalf of another. Prayer in favor of another. An intercessor reminds the Lord of His promises until they are fulfilled. We must always be cognizant of what we know and believe about God in our hearts. We must know His promises found in scripture. Christ intercedes for us as our advocate in heaven. We must stand in between the people of God and their problems to protect and plead for mercy for our people.

All of humanity is on my heart because I was once in darkness, and somebody interceded on my behalf. Intercession is the divine weapon of mercy and power to defeat darkness. God will destroy the works of darkness through our intercession and destroy strongholds. He will be merciful to those who do not deserve mercy. We must cry out to Him!

To grow in our effectiveness as intercessors, we should always desire to grow in God's knowledge. We must grow in our understanding of His character so we can represent Him in our daily walk. We must grow our understanding of who we are and what our authority is in Christ when we stand before our Lord in intercession.

That is my stratagem; Prayer and to pray without ceasing for the people of our God.

About The Author:

Sheneki (Nikki) White was born to the proud parents of Willie and Nancy (Parker) White. Nikki's pride and joy are her two beloved daughters, Misha and Demitria, and her adored 3-year-old grandson Khalil. Being raised in a Baptist church with her mother alongside her brothers, Nikki received the gift of salvation at an early age and entered her intimate relationship with the Lord in her adult life. Nikki, to this day, still thanks her dearest mother for introducing the Lord to her at a very young age.

Nikki joined the military at the young age of 17 and, shortly after, was deployed to Saudi Arabia, Operation Desert Storm, known as the first Gulf War. Being deployed to act in the war had never crossed Nikki's mind. Knowing how our protector Jehovah Nissi bought her through such a terrifying waging war that had left her shell shocked and suffering from PTSD, has increased her faith and a burning desire to go after God's own heart.

Nikki's purpose is to effectively intercede on behalf of others and pray against the spiritual battles we all face.
Nikki exercises her authority of power according to scripture: Luke 10:19 NLT "*Look I have given you authority over all the power of the enemy, and you can walk among snakes and scorpions and crush them. Nothing will harm you.*"

Contact Info: Facebook.com/nikki.white.9862273

Strategic Military Power

"Directing Military Power"

Explains the use of creativity and timing in building an army's momentum

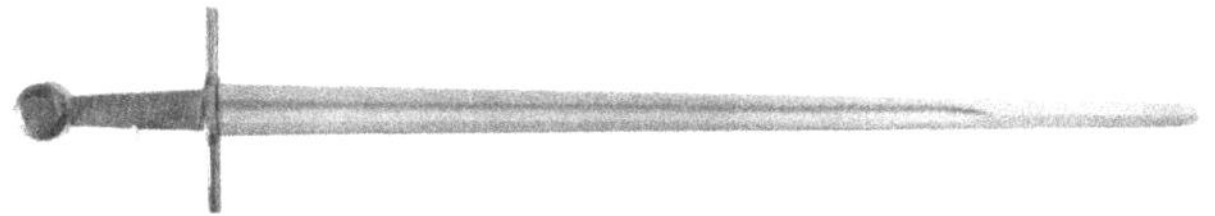

ZANDRA OSBORNE

Chapter 13

The Strategies Of A Militant Warrior

In most wars, many soldiers are equipped and trained in knowing how to be prepared for war, thus becoming militant warriors. A militant person is one who uses aggressively combative and strategic methods in pursuit of an objective. A Warrior is a brave or experienced soldier or fighter. Normal civilians become trained, militant warriors for the purpose of necessary battle when enlisted in one of the five military branches. Collectively, these two characteristics create a person who can withstand and fight against any enemy's tactics with their newfound training in war. Special Operations in the military branches may enact a soldier with a special skill called a Sniper. This soldier is precisely trained and skilled in pinpointing a target to eliminate the enemy's threat with one shot. In the spiritual realm, A sniper is a highly trained soldier who specializes in targeting the true intent of demonic forces. In this war of good and evil, every warrior must enact their strategic training as militant warriors to defeat the enemy.

Joshua was an esteemed leader and warrior who was trained under Moses and led one of the biggest conquests of Canaan. He established peace for the twelve tribes and appointed boundaries. "By faith, the walls of Jericho fell, after they were compassed about for seven days. By Faith, the harlot Ra-hab perished not with them that believed not when she received the spies with peace" (Hebrews 11:30-31 KJV). Joshua was a militant warrior who was prepared to help build and accepted his assignment as commander of the Israelites. He picked up where Moses left off and led the twelve tribes across the promised land. "Through faith they subdued kingdoms, worked righteousness, obtained promises, stopped the mouths of lions, quenched the violence of fire, escaped the edge of the sword, out of weakness they were made strong, waxed valiant in fight, turned to fight the armies of the aliens" (Hebrews 11:33-34). Joshua was a faithful warrior and mentee, who watched Moses move the Israelites out of Egypt. Who is your mentor? Joshua was obedient to Moses' orders and was faithful to God's commands.

What strategies did Joshua use that made him a

militant warrior? What methods did he apply that made him God's valiant and effective military leader?

First, Joshua was **confrontational** in his approach. He was not afraid to attack his enemy until utter destruction and demise. In other words, he did not show signs of backing up or backing down in battle.

"Now when Joshua was near Jericho, he looked up and saw a man standing in front of him with a drawn sword in his hand. Joshua went up to him and asked, "Are you for us or for our enemies?" (Joshua 5:13 NIV)

"Then the LORD said to Joshua, "Do not be afraid; do not be discouraged. Take the whole army with you and go up and attack Ai. For I have delivered into your hands the king of Ai, his people, his city and his land. (Joshua 8:1 NIV)"

Second, Joshua was **courageous** in his position. Joshua showed strength and courage and gained triumph over his enemies despite opposition in the form of pressure, threats, and intimidation from violent enemies.

"Have I not commanded you? Be strong and courageous. Do not be afraid; do not be discouraged, for the Lord your God will be with you wherever you go." (Joshua 1:9 NIV)
"The LORD said to Joshua, "Do not be afraid of them; I have given them into your hand. Not one of them will be able to withstand you." (Joshua 10:8 NIV)

Third, Joshua was **committed** to the fulfillment of his assignment. He did not quit in the middle of the battle and ran. Nor did he forfeit, retreat, or hand over the victory to the opposition.

"The Lord said to Joshua, "Do not be afraid of them, because by this time tomorrow I will hand all of them, slain, over to Israel. You are to hamstring their horses and burn their chariots." (Joshua 11:6 NIV)

"Joshua did to them as the Lord had directed: He hamstrung their horses and burned their chariots." (Joshua 11:9 NIV)

To all militant warriors, I charge you this day to apply these methods in warfare. Sharpen your weapons and move speed ahead. You have what it takes to attack and conquer! In your movement, DO NOT move or act in your emotions.

Throughout my life as a trained leader, I became a

sniper in the spirit realm. I became a militant warrior when I overcame the Spirit of Rejection. However, once I started to embrace who I was and identify myself in the spirit realm, nothing else mattered, including the rejection of others. Rejection occurs when a person or group of people exclude an individual. This person or group refuses to acknowledge or accept the individual's presence, contributions, or ideas. My prayer for you is to learn how to obey God's voice and never react to what you see or what you have heard. Learn yourself, so you know your identity. "As you come to him, the Living Stone, rejected by humans but chosen by God and precious to him." (I Peter 2:4 NIV).

About The Author:

Prophetess Zandra Osborne is an author and ordained minister. She is the founder of Eagle Wings Faith Ministries. Her goal is to help others be birthed into their God given assignments. Always remember, "Only what you do for Christ shall last."
Learn more about Zandra: Facebook: Author Zandra

Jackson-Osborne & Midwife Sessions

Email: zandra72801@yahoo.com

Facebook: Author Zandra Jackson-Osborne & Midwife Sessions
Instagram: midwife_ sessions
Email: zandra72801@yahoo.com

Strategic Military Power

"Directing Military Power"

Explains the use of creativity and timing in building an army's momentum

QUENTINA ATTIPOE

Chapter 14

The Strategy of the Beloved

I cannot lead you where I have not or am not willing to go... Let me share with you, where I have been.

I have been to the pits of hell to rescue abused and neglected children, I have been to the courtroom to advocate for the welfare of children and to intervene for parents who have done their best. I have been where children are starving, while fathers and mothers cry helplessly. I have sat alongside an addict feening for his next fix; and there, as he experiences withdraws because he did not get one. I have been by the side of the desperate wife crying out to have her marriage restored, and the grieving mother longing for her child to be home.

The theater had been SET and I was to REMAIN in that place… it was then TIME… as it is now to WAGE WAR!

Our greatest intercessor, Jesus, teaches us to "wage war" from the place and position of peace and love.[1] It is from that place and position that the intercessor wages war. It is from that place and position the intentional strategies are employed and deployed. All the weapons needed to successfully fight any battle are already in your hands. Whether you are a new intercessor, or a seasoned veteran, the weapons for success and victory are within you, as with

---

1 Matthew 26:64; Mark 14:62

all children of God.[2] All of the weapons needed for your battle are found in the place and utilized from that position. The place is the Throne Room, that place from where your "Abba Father" rules and reigns. The position is seated with Jesus, the Christ, as a joint heir of the Kingdom.[3]

Strategy: Remain In Place and Position

This is what I have learned while in my correct place and position.

Strategy of intercession must be purposeful. The purpose of intercession is found in the heart of our Heavenly Father. The tactics and plan needed are in the mind of God, and He desires to share them with me and you.[4] Without knowing the heart and commands of our

---

[2] Psalm 18:25-50, 35:1-28, 149:1-9; Luke 11:5-13; Romans 13:8-14; 2 Corinthians 10:2-6

[3] Romans 8:12-17; Ephesians 3:5-6

[4] Luke 10:21-22

Heavenly Father regarding a matter, one prays amiss.[5] The intercessor must seek first the heart of the Father. It is then He will add all the Kingdom's dimensions to our prayers. Beginning my prayer with worship and adoration, I become open to hearing the voice of my Abba Father.

In that place of intimacy, I know how much I am loved and how much my Father loves the subject of prayers.[6] My prayer begins to reflect my Father's heart for that individual for which I am praying, not the circumstance. My prayers decree and declare His desires for that individual, that their situation and trial birth within him or her the desire to know His heart and long for His presence, for it is His presence that changes the thing. As I pray for leaders and government, my desire for the people of that nation to know the intimacy of my Father's presence

---

5 James 4:3

6 John 3:16-17, 15:9-17

grows. The prayer of the intercessor should reflect the heart of the Father into the earth, bringing the light of Jesus to illuminate the understanding of His people.[7]

Strategy: Pray The Father's

I was taught that being an intercessor meant that I was "standing in the GAP" for those I pray. My intercession was blocking God's wrath or judgement from occurring to that person, group, or nation. When a child is in constant fear of the wrath, abuse reveals trauma of the parent. Our Heavenly Father is love and wants His children to know His love for them.[8] It is His love and goodness that draws all people to Himself. What I have learned in my spiritual "boot camp" is that I not only stand in but become the A-"*GAP*"-E of my Father in the circumstance.

---

7 Matthew 5:14-15; Mark 4:21-25; Luke 8:16-18; John 8:12, 12:46

8 John 3:16-17

We declare through the cross and blood of Jesus, we have access granted through the Throne Room of Heaven and to our Abba Father.[9] It is being seated with My Father that I have learned through the Father's AGAPE love... ACCESS is GRANTED, and POWER is ENDOWED. Not only is power, or ability, to get through the circumstance, but the wisdom and endurance is found in Him. It is also in the ACCESS GRANTED that PROVISION is also ENDOWED by My Father. Provision for every need and concern for which you and I intercede is granted.

Strategy: Become The Agape Love Of Your Father

It is not until we enter into the presence of our Abba Father consistently that you and I discover the peace, rest, and safety. It is from that position which war of

---

9 Galatians 4:6-7; Ephesians 2:18-22, 3:12-13

intercession is waged. You and I, as joint heirs, are SEATED in heavenly places with Jesus.[10] Our position is there. I have learned that, as I intercede, I simply remind my Heaven Father what He has already said and established in His Word and through His Word, Jesus. I become that Beloved Daughter of the King that can ask what she will, and it SHALL be given unto her.[11] When I recognize that my position as a daughter of the Creator has authority and that His love for me is the power, mighty things happen. His love for me encompasses every individual (His Creation) impacted by whatever the circumstance no matter how horrific it may be. I have learned to pray in rhythm to my Father's heartbeat of agape love.

People who do not know the Heart of the Father;

---

10 Acts 5:30-32; Ephesians 2:4-10; Revelation 4:2-3

11 Matthew 6:33; Colossians 2:2-3

therefore, many perish for a lack of knowledge of it. People do not know who they are, nor whose they are; therefore, they perish for the lack of not knowing.[12] Learning this has changed the strategy in which I enter intercession…

Strategy: Know That You Are Beloved

Jesus went to the one that was crippled and hurting like the man at the pool of Bethesda, overlooked like Zacchaeus, and outcast like the demoniac.[13] He went to them, intentionally positioning Himself for an encounter to occur. I have learned that intercession is a legal term enforcing action of recovery or restoration. Its root is derived from *cessavit*, "a writ given by statute to recover land that the tenant has failed to perform the conditions of his tenure".[14] My intercession requires action to take place.

---

12 Hosea 4:6

13 John 5:1-15; Luke 19:1-9; Matthew 8:23-34

14 https://www.thefreedictionary.com/Cessavit

My actions must reflect my intercession.

I have also learned that My Father gives strategy daily.[15] In many ways, Our Father reveals the hearts of men and women. Whether it is in the words that he says… the look that she gives… wounded hearts are being revealed. My intercession does not always occur in my secret place of prayer, but as I look into the eyes of the one that My Father loves so deeply that He has asked me to lay my life down at that moment. Because I follow the example of my Savior, I might at any time be called to lay my life down in that moment to become A-"*GAP*"-E to be the bridge that My Father may use to reach that one.[16] My strategy for intercession then becomes a "repairer of the breach" and ushers the presence and love of Our Lord to that wounded individual.[17] I may do this in a kind word, listening ear, or

---

15 Psalm 27:4-8, 105:3-4; Luke 12:22-34

16 John 10:11-18; 1 John 3:1-24

17 Isaiah 58:1-14

providing for a need. My intercession becomes my acts of service. Intercession becomes my lifestyle, as continually I live in My Father's presence.

Strategy: Let Your Life Become The Intercession

Through my personal journey of restoration and transformation, I have learned to be an intercessor who remains seated in heavenly places in the presence of Jesus and My Abba Father. I have learned to receive the love of My Abba Father and my identity as His Beloved Daughter. It is from that place that I become the agape love of My Father. I come alongside others, both lost and found, to lead them to the place of healing and transformation in the presence of My Abba Father.

About The Author:

Beloved daughter of our most high God, Quentina Maria Attipoe, is a cherished wife and blessed mother of a blended family. In partnership with The Lord, she and her husband, Edmond, co-founded AGAPE Ghana in 2019, a ministry which provides individuals and families assistance with access to medical, social, and educational services. In 2020, AGAPE Worldwide, Inc. was established to expand assistance to other nations, beginning in Uganda.

Contact Quentina Attipoe:
QMPJAttipoe@outlook.com
AGAPEGhana@outlook.com
AGAPEGhana.org
FB: AGAPE Ghana (@qmpjagape)

www.ingramcontent.com/pod-product-compliance
Ingram Content Group UK Ltd.
Pitfield, Milton Keynes, MK11 3LW, UK
UKHW020141250726
13967UKWH00002B/799

9 781716 257230